Realistic Devotions for Teens

SO-DFK-969

Artificial Flavors-
100% Friendship

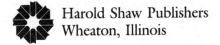

Harold Shaw Publishers
Wheaton, Illinois

JEFF and RAMONA TUCKER

To
Mom and Dad Cramer
who lovingly give us
the best gift of all—
their friendship.

A very special thanks to the following people: Evangeline and Brian, who have shown us that family can be best friends; Jack ("Punkin"), our co-youth-group-leader who has given his time, energy, and best of all—his heart; Corinne and Char for their help in creative brainstorming; HFC youth group for their love, concern, and spirit of unity (and for good-naturedly allowing us to use them as guinea pigs for the material in this book!).

Unless otherwise noted, all Scripture references are taken from the *New International Version*, copyright © 1978 by the New York Bible Society. Used by permission.

Copyright © 1989, Jeffrey Tucker & Ramona Cramer Tucker

ISBN 0-87788-582-6

Cover and interior design: K. L. Mulder
Cover photo: Jim Whitmer

Library of Congress Cataloging-in-Publication Data

Tucker, Jeff, 1960—
  No artificial flavors.
  1. Teenagers—Prayer—Books and devotions—English.
2. Friendship—Juvenile literature.   I. Tucker, Ramona, 1962—
II. Title.
BV4850.T83   1989   241'.646   88-34710
ISBN 0-87788-582-6

98 97 96 95 94 93 92 91 90 89
10 9 8 7 6 5 4 3 2 1

☐ CONTENTS

☐ CHECK IT OUT

When we asked the teens in our youth group to write down the three things that were most important to them, two tied for the #1 place—friends and family. School or peer pressure, which also has to do with friendship, took third!

In "Friends Are Friends Forever," Michael W. Smith sings, "And friends are friends forever, if the Lord is the Lord of them . . . a lifetime's not too long to live as friends." What a beautiful tribute to friendship! But are friends really that—forever friends? We'll take a look at that question along with many others.

Being a teen isn't easy—we know. You're faced with more concerns than ever before—peer pressure, self-esteem, romance, family problems, questions about whether God is really there or not. Maybe you're confused about who you are and just how you fit into this crazy, topsy-turvy world. Or perhaps you're lonely. You might have lots of "friends," but you still feel like you're in a locker all by yourself, and someone slammed the door.

Together we'll look at different types of friendships to discover tips for making the good ones last and for breaking off the not-so-good ones. And as we share the stories of the kids in this book, you'll find help for areas you're struggling in. Things like how to handle pesky siblings and snobby cliques; how to forgive—and forget—friends when they drop you on the floor; how to solve sticky conflicts. We'll even look at the importance of guy/girl friendships and what's different about boy friends and boyfriends.

In these pages, you'll find space to scribble in, friendly suggestions for activities, and things to think or pray about during the rest of the day. Nothing would make us happier than to see this book well-worn and stained with your scribbles, thoughts, and discoveries.

But overall, we pray that you'll discover—in this book and in the pages of Scripture—a Friend who's got all the #1 qualities you could ever want or need. We'll let you fill in the name!

Jeff & Ramona

More or Less?

☐ DAY ONE

Friendship Power

T ina was exasperated. She and Chris were at it again. She felt like throwing him and all his stubborn ideas right out the school window. Friends were supposed to stick together like chewing gum and desks, right? And think and act like twins?

Tina and Chris had been good friends for two years; they'd been drawn together like magnets. But lately she and Chris always rubbed each other the wrong way. Tina's family was conservative—they thought Amy Grant's first album was super-rocky and obnoxious. Her curfew was at ten every night, even weekends.

Chris was almost exactly her opposite. He listened to Stryper and Rez band and really got into it. His parents didn't even set a curfew. They said they trusted him to make his own wise decisions. Tina and Chris were always knocking heads over that one, wondering, "So who's right anyway?"

They disagreed on a lot of other issues too.

Do Opposites Really Attract?

Friendship isn't automatic. You don't just push a button on the Perfect Friendship Machine and k-chink! Out falls a perfect, made-to-your-order friend. Actually, that would be pretty boring. You don't need a duplicate copy of yourself as a friend—it would be like staring at yourself every day.

Friendship doesn't always mean agreeing and being clones of each other. Differences can be good. They make us think and help us grow as persons. And they make us stronger persons because we have to make our own decisions. Good friends learn to compromise and to give each other freedom to be who they are. They are dedicated to each other and to learning how to make their relationship work. Good friends let each other be unique, and they challenge each other to become the super-duper best they can be.

Unlikely People

Some of the most unlikely people in the Bible were friends. Take Moses and Aaron for example. Moses was a terrific organizer; God needed his talent when the Israelites were wandering in the desert. But Moses had a problem. He couldn't speak well—he'd get so nervous he'd stumble and stutter over his words. He needed his brother Aaron who was a great speaker, but tended to go off the deep end when Moses wasn't around. (When Moses trekked up the mountain to get the ten commandments, Aaron allowed the people to do a major no-no—build a golden calf to worship instead of God.)

Together Moses and Aaron were dynamos. And what's more, they were even real live brothers! That's a pretty good example of what working together can do.

Two other friends who worked together at a task were Elijah and Elisha. A poor guy, Elijah was always running around the country without a roof over his head. Elisha, on the other hand, had five oxen (in Bible times that meant he was a lot better off). Today it would be like Elijah having a Yugo while Elisha had a red Porsche 930 Turbo.

Even though they were about as far apart in social position and money as you could get, they still became close friends. They realized that differences were necessary and normal, but that each one of them still had a special place in God's plan.

Paul explained it in Romans 12:4-6a:

Just as each of us has one body with many members, and these members do not all have the same function, so in Christ we who are many form one body, and each member belongs to all the others. We have different gifts, according to the grace given us.

4

Like & Unlike

Evaluate your three closest friends. How are they like you?

_____

_____

_____

Different from you?

_____

_____

_____

Thank God today for giving you unique friends, and for giving you such a special place in his plans.

☐ DAY TWO

Belly Button Fuzz & All That Stuff

D ad was on the warpath again. In fact, he seemed to be yelling even more than usual—which was most of the time.

Trish sighed. She and Dad could never agree on anything. Lately Trish had worked especially hard to keep her room clean and to help around the house but Dad didn't seem to notice. Even when she did something extra, like washing Dad's car, Dad always found something wrong with it.

She felt like she couldn't even talk to him anymore. Whenever he came home, *if* he came home, he was drunk. And then when he got home, he'd have a drink in his hand within five minutes. She was tired of hearing her parents fight. They even fought when her friends came over. It was so embarrassing that she didn't ask anyone to come over anymore.

Except Candi. Candi was her always-there friend. They did everything together—worked at Burger King after school on Mondays and Wednesdays, sang in choir on Sundays, and went out together on weekends. They shared everything, down to diet Cokes and pocket change. When Trish's dad yelled, Candi didn't get embarrassed like Trish's other friends did. She just rolled her eyes and smiled that twinkly smile that made Trish feel immediately better. Candi understood and loved her just the same, alcoholic dad and all. She trusted Candi completely. Candi would do anything for her—she was that kind of friend.

A Loyal Friend

Candi was a loyal friend, both in time and heart. It didn't matter to her one bit that Trish had a rough home life. She just took it in stride and went right on being a heart friend.

David and Jonathan had a loyal friendship like that. Even though they lived a long time ago, there are a lot of things we can learn from them. Jonathan was the son of a king, and David was only a shepherd boy. But that didn't stop them from being friends. Can you imagine? It's like the poorest kid in school with the rattiest clothes becoming the best friend of the richest, best-looking kid with all the name-brand clothes and a mansion of a house.

Brotherly Love

David and Jonathan had a special friendship. They grew to love each other like brothers, and they stuck together through thick and thin. You can read the story of their loyal friendship in 1 Samuel chapters 19 and 20.

The Bible says this about faithful friends:

> *Be devoted to one another in brotherly love. Honor one another above yourselves. Never be lacking in zeal, but keep your spiritual fervor, serving the Lord. Be joyful in hope, patient in affliction, faithful in prayer. Share with God's people who are in need. Practice hospitality.* Romans 12:10-14

Old Faithful

Do you have a special friend you feel like you can always count on? Why do you feel that way?

_____

_____

Are you a faithful, loyal friend? What can you do this week to become one?

_____

_____

☐ DAY THREE

Even When the Truth Hurts

I can't believe it! Tim muttered to himself as he plopped on his unmade bed. *Bruce is supposed to be a Christian!* Tim was ticked off. He had thought Bruce was a cool guy. He didn't wear the word SUPER CHRISTIAN plastered in capital letters across his chest or anything like that, but he was—well— something else.

But lately things had changed. Tim's group of friends seemed no longer good enough for Bruce. And today at school, he'd heard that Bruce got drunk last night.

What good is all this stuff he told me about Christ anyway? It doesn't seem to make any difference to him now! Tim thought. He felt like phoning Bruce. After all, they *had* been good friends. And shouldn't friends be honest with each other?

He reached for the phone. But then he wondered, *What if he gets mad when I ask him what he's up to? Or worse, what if he laughs at me?* Slamming down the phone, Tim dropped his chin into his hands. *I'm such a chicken*, he thought.

A Shot in the Arm

Bruce isn't the only one who needs a good buddy to turn him around. We all need it sometimes. Maybe we aren't doing something radical like getting drunk, but there are other things—like gossiping, having a bad attitude, or ignoring the new kid.

8

In Isaiah 38-39, we read a great story about two friends—Isaiah the prophet and Hezekiah the king. Hezekiah was a good guy, but he was also human. He made a big mistake. When the king of Babylon sent him a get-well present, it went to his head. He was so pleased that he showed the Babylonians (his country's enemies) where all his gold and silver and other treasures were. It was like showing a robber where you keep your piggy bank.

Hezekiah didn't think past his own emotions to what he was doing to his kingdom and the people. When Isaiah heard about it, he marched directly to the king and confronted him, telling Hezekiah that because of what he had done, the Babylonians would invade the country and carry its people and treasures into captivity.

It Takes Guts

Isaiah was one gutsy dude. Even though the king could have anyone executed that he wanted to, Isaiah wasn't afraid. What meant more to Isaiah was keeping a covenant of honesty with his friend—even when his friend got off on the wrong track.

Most likely, none of your friends are going to have you executed, even if they get mad enough! But you may feel like it. They might turn you off or go on doing what they are doing anyway. But God calls us to keep our friends accountable in their faith:

> *Two are better than one . . . If one falls down, his friend can help him up. But pity the man who falls and has no one to help him up! Though one may be overpowered, two can defend themselves. A cord of three strands is not quickly broken.* Ecclesiastes 4:9-10, 12

Good Medicine

When was the last time you told a friend the truth about something good in his life? Something bad?

_____

_____

Good friends hold each other accountable. Make a covenant with a friend to be honest with each other—even when the truth hurts.

☐ DAY FOUR

Tough as Toenails

It was 3 o'clock, and the school bell zinged through Terrin High. Randy grabbed his books and tore down the hallway, raced down the long steps and out to his beat-up Mustang. *All right! Freedom at last!* He cranked up his radio.

He was going to see Brian, his best football buddy—he'd agreed to bring his assignments over since Brian was stuck in bed. A week ago, Brian had been tackled and went down pretty hard. He broke his arm and his leg in five places. *What a bummer!* Randy thought. *I'd hate it if it were me.*

Then the months turned into winter. Going over to Brian's every day started to get a little old. *How far does this friendship thing go anyway?* Randy wondered, shivering even with his turned-up collar. *You know, I need some time of my own. I didn't know it would take this much work or time. I'd really like to go out with the guys tonight and here I am, stuck going over to Brian's house again.*

A Committed Friend

Maybe you're like Randy. You're starting to feel like one of your friends is a real burden—too possessive of your time, or always down, or, like Brian, sick and out of commission. Sometimes you feel like blowing your friend off.

If anyone had a good reason to dump a friend, it was Jonathan. All the odds were against David. Jonathan's dad, King Saul, was really angry at David. Once Saul was so mad that he even threw a spear at David and tried to pin him to the wall!

When the Going Gets Tough

But that didn't stop Jonathan. When the going got tough, Jonathan got tougher. He helped David hide from Saul and devised a plan to find out if his dad really intended to kill David. (See 1 Samuel 20). Jonathan risked the king's anger and got it. His dad even threw a spear at him!

Probably no one will ever throw an actual spear at you—spears went out with the Dark Ages and cannibals. But people might throw other spears at you. Things like, "How come you're hanging out with that guy? He's really weird." Or, "You're still *her* friend? Well, then, you can't be *my* friend." Then you have to decide if you will be a committed friend no matter what.

The Bible says this about a committed friend:

A man of many companions
may come to ruin,
but there is a friend
who sticks closer than a brother. Proverbs 18:24

Paraphrased, this verse means "indiscriminately chosen friends may bring trouble, but a genuine friend sticks with you through thick and thin" (Ryrie NASB, study notes). A genuine friend—like David, like Jonathan.

Sticking Together

What does being a committed friend mean to you?

_____

_____

Choose one friend. Pray that God will help you put your ideas about commitment into action this week.

☐ DAY FIVE

Success Story

Amy was a cute, petite blonde—a junior at Glendale West. The only problem was, she'd transferred in from a school in Alabama.

Amy felt lost. Every day she dreaded going to school. The first day was the worst. Wandering down the hallways, she'd been looking for her English room. All of a sudden, a kid yelled at her, "Hey, frosh! You're not supposed to be in this hall. It's a SENIOR hall. Get lost!" She'd walked away with all the dignity she could muster.

Living in the north was very different. Everything moved a lot faster, and kids weren't as friendly. Or maybe it seemed that way because she didn't know anyone. She was too scared to open her mouth, because if she did, everyone would know she was different. She'd lived in Alabama all her life, and she hadn't realized she had an accent until she moved to Ohio.

The first two months passed slowly. She still didn't have any friends. Between classes she walked alone, and she sat alone at lunch.

One Friday after school, she rushed home and up to her room. "I hate this place! Why did Mom have to move here anyway? No one likes me!" she yelled and threw herself on her bed. Then the tears came—a whole hour of them. Her eyes looked puffy even the next day.

It's Up to You

How do you choose your friends? Sometimes it just happens, and you don't feel like you really *chose* anybody. Other times, maybe you're like Amy. You have a hard time reaching out beyond yourself even to say "Hi y'all!" Maybe you feel insecure, and you wish that someone would just say hi and invite you out for a Coke.

But in order to have friends, you need to ask yourself, "What kind of friend do you want to be?" Friendship is more than *finding* the right person; it's *becoming* the right person.

Essentials

This week you've been thinking about some essential qualities of friendship—valuing people and their differences, loyalty, trust, honesty, commitment. Of course there are lots more, and we'll be discovering more in our next weeks together, but these make a starting place.

If you focus on becoming loyal, trustworthy, and committed instead of groaning that you don't have friends, you might discover a few surprises.

The Bible says this:

> *Therefore, strengthen your feeble arms and weak knees. "Make level paths for your feet," so that the lame may not be disabled, but rather healed.* Hebrews 12:12-13

You can either focus on your own loneliness and sink deeper into it, or you can look around and try to meet some of the needs that other people have. If you're concentrating on helping someone else, you won't have time to be self-conscious.

You'll find that you start caring more about other people. And guess what? They'll begin to realize what a good friend you are! Having a committed friend is the best!

Self-Check

Copy this verse and put it in your locker, your mirror, your car— some place where you will see it every day:

If we love one another, God lives in us and his love is made complete in us. And he has given us this command: Whoever loves God must also love his brother. 1 John 4:12, 21

Keep asking yourself, "What kind of friend do you want to be?" Remember—your success story is up to you.

School
Snapshots

☐ DAY ONE

Shy
Shari

I t was the first day of Shari's sophomore year. She walked down the beige hallways, glancing to the left and then to the right. Her locker was here somewhere.

Where is #292? she wondered. She found #250 and #280, and then she saw them—the 290's. They were surrounded by a whole bunch of laughing guys and girls.

Shari's heart sank. Her head drooped as she hid behind her new notebook and oozed past her locker. She rounded the corner and pretended to take a long drink from the water fountain, anything to kill time. When she walked back to her locker, no one was there. Relieved, she opened the door and slid in her jacket.

What's my problem anyway? she muttered, ticked off at herself.

Then the bell rang. *Great!* She was late for class—and what was worse, late on the very first day! Now she'd have to walk in and find her seat in front of everybody. Shari felt like crawling in her locker and shutting the door—permanently.

Locker Acrobatics

Maybe you're like Shari. You get so nervous when someone talks to you that you slam your thumb in your locker or drop your books (on *their* feet of course!). Or maybe you feel like you're ugly because you have truckloads of pimples, and you just don't want to be noticed until the Clearasil has done its job. Sometimes you don't feel you're good enough to be noticed because you're not pretty, or handsome, or even above average in anything.

Looking Beyond

Shari always spent an hour in the bathroom every morning getting her makeup just perfect. Finally her father asked her, "Why are you so concerned about the way you look?"

"Because everyone will be looking at me when I get out of the car," she replied, matter-of-factly.

"So you think that you are center stage and that everyone is looking at you, right? I think that's pretty prideful."

Shari was shocked. She'd never thought of it in that way before. She knew she was shy, but she never thought she was proud.

Maybe you haven't thought about it that way either. A lot of people are busy looking at themselves.

Plucking Up Courage

After the Israelites wandered in the desert for forty years, Moses died. God appointed Joshua as the new leader and told him:

> *As I was with Moses, so I will be with you; I will never leave you nor forsake you . . . Be strong and courageous. Do not be terrified; do not be discouraged, for the LORD your God will be with you wherever you go.* Joshua 1:5b, 9

If God could do that for Joshua, who was in charge of thousands of people, he can do it for you, too! The next time you feel like dogfood (and maybe think you look like it), reread that verse.

Who do you know who's like Shy Shari? (Maybe it's *you.*) Make some notes about what you could say to him or her this week.

Write yourself this reminder note with big capital letters:

GOD WANTS ME TO S-T-R-E-T-C-H!

Then put it in your pocket or notebook to encourage you to reach out when you're having a hard time doing just that.

18

☐ DAY TWO

Toss-aside
Tim

"**H**ey Tim!" Jerry's voice boomed across the parking lot. "How was your date with Colleen last night?"

"Terrific!" Tim grinned, showing perfect white teeth. "She's a neat girl." He slicked his nut-brown hair back. It fell into perfect waves.

All the girls thought Tim was Hunk-of-the-year. Always perfectly dressed in the right clothes, he was the biggest stud of Fremont High. And he knew it.

"Are you going out with her again?" Jerry asked.

"Naw. She's O.K. and everything, but really not my type." And Tim went on to explain for five minutes why she wasn't.

Tim treated everyone alike—it didn't matter whether they were guys or girls. He was a be-a-friend-once-and-then-toss-aside guy. *Why shouldn't he?* he figured. *He had his pick of anyone he wanted to be friends with. They were all at his feet, begging to be his friend because he was such a cool guy and all.*

Jerry shook his head. He just couldn't understand Tim.

Straight to the Head

Perfect Tim. He was a popular guy. The only problem was he let it go straight to his head. Ever heard the saying, "His head's so fat he couldn't get it through the doorway?" Well, Tim's was so big it could have taken over the world—or at least his world, Fremont High.

Right now it's cool to be like Tim. But sooner or later, Tim's going to fall over his own feet and splat! There goes the reputation. Suddenly he won't seem so handsome anymore. You can't toss people aside or treat them like objects for long. Soon they won't want to be around you.

Attitude Check

In Philippians 2:3-4, Paul says,

> *Do nothing out of selfish ambition or vain conceit, but in humility consider others better than yourselves. Each of you should look not only to your own interests, but also to the interests of others.*

Evaluate yourself honestly. How do you treat other kids at school?

_____

_____

Write down examples from specific situations that you would like to change.

_____

_____

Ask God to help you treat others the way you would want to be treated.

☐ DAY THREE

Merry
Mary

"**G**ood morning, Joy! Isn't it just be-e-eautiful today? I love spring and flowers and sunshine and *everything*, don't you?" Mary gushed.

Joy groaned. Every morning it was the same scene. She felt like ducking back under her covers and hiding. Since Mary was also a junior and lived on her block, she had taken it upon herself to walk with Joy to school every day.

This is disgusting! Go away! Joy exclaimed inside.

Mary bubbled, "I just couldn't wait to get up today so I could wear my new jeans to school. The girls are going to love them, don't you think?"

Joy propped open her blue eyes—just a corner though. Enough to see Mary perched on the edge of her bed, looking 110% awake and ready to go, as usual.

Joy sighed and dragged herself up in a fog while Mary chattered on happily. *She can't be this happy all the time! It's impossible!* Joy thought. Joy put on a semi-smile while she threw on her jeans and a rumpled *Chicago* t-shirt.

Blowing the Bubble

We all know someone like Merry Mary. Maybe it's the girl at school who is always so bubbly that you want to smash her because *nobody* could be that happy all the time. Or maybe it's the guy who's the clown of the class, who laughs even when the other kids give him a hard time.

Merry Mary may have always seemed happy on the outside, but what was happening on the inside? What Joy didn't know was that Mary's parents were breaking up. Every night they fought. It echoed in Mary's brain. Scared they'd get a divorce and yet wanting the screaming to end, Mary felt caught—and guilty. She wondered if it was her fault.

The up-front happy stuff was just a big fake. Too embarrassed to tell anyone what was going on at home, Mary hid her problems.

Real People

No matter what people act like, you have to look beyond their words and actions to what they are really thinking and feeling. Maybe they need you to ask, "How are you *really* doing?" and to take time for them. They need you to show that you care about them and are interested in them *personally*. In Galatians, Paul encourages us to keep doing good for others:

> Let us not become weary in doing good, for at the proper time we will reap a harvest if we do not give up. Therefore, as we have opportunity, let us do good to all people, especially to those who belong to the family of believers. Galatians 6:9-10

If someone is happy, it doesn't always mean that they have personal problems. But be sensitive. You might be surprised what you find out when you keep your eyes and ears open.

Writing Tip

Write a kind note to a Merry Mary this week. Practice here.

_____

_____

If you're shy about it, you don't even have to sign it. Just be encouraging and sensitive. Ask Jesus to give you a new, special love for the Merry Marys in your life.

☐ DAY FOUR

Tunnel Ted

T ed was Mr. Average in just about everything. But he could be considered almost handsome—until he opened his mouth that is. Then he bored everyone to death.

Ted was at it again. Andrea could tell that he was interested in her, and she sort of liked him. So she had invited him over to her house yesterday after school. He'd even offered to carry her books. She couldn't believe it! He was so-o-o nice.

Then he blew it. Big time. When they climbed Andrea's front porch steps, they'd run into her brother Brian. Both Brian and Ted were into cars. And not just into them—they breathed, ate, and slept cars. Talking about engines to them was like eating chocolate chip cookies to Andrea. They had spent two hours talking about turbo chargers and dual exhausts, and finally took off to see Brian's black 85 SS Monte Carlo in the garage, leaving Andrea slumped and bored on the porch.

She hadn't even seen Ted the rest of the evening. He'd waved goodbye and yelled happily, "Hey, thanks for inviting me!"

Today Ted was at her locker again. "Andrea, your brother is terrific! And he knows so much." Ted launched off into lingo about boosting his car's horsepower again. Andrea felt like screaming.

One-Track Minds

Everyone knows a one-focused guy or girl. Maybe like Ted, the car expert, he talks about cars every time one rolls by. When you try to switch the subject, he looks at you blankly like you don't exist. Maybe it's Lori, whose mind holds only visions of Jordache jeans and Stratford Mall. Or Bob, the Bible banger whose Bible is so big he can't even stuff it in his locker.

When these people are around, you probably feel like killing them (even if you're a good kid and the thought of murder would never enter your mind). They always seem to crank their mouths in gear, but rarely their ears.

Switching Tracks

What words do you think describe one-track people? Maybe selfish, insensitive. But have you ever thought that maybe they just don't know what else to talk about? They feel insecure, so they pick one subject that they know more about than anyone else. Or they could be genuinely interested in a certain subject and honestly don't know they are boring you to death.

But you know what? If you really choose to listen and actually show interest, you might learn something. Even better, they might realize they have a genuine friend in you and start listening to what *you* have to say.

The Bible encourages us to put guts behind what we say and do:

> *Dear Children, let us not love with words or tongue but with actions and in truth.* 1 John 3:18

How 'Bout You?

Are you like Ted? Wanting to talk only about the things you're interested in? Do you get bored easily? Make notes here about your last two conversations today. (If you can't remember them, maybe that's a clue about your listening powers!)

_____

_____

This week, when someone is boring you, turn your ears on and your Walkman off. You might learn something about them or even yourself! Ask God to make you a more sensitive listener.

☐ DAY FIVE

Can't-Make-Up-My-Mind Carol

"Hey, Carol! Are you going to Shelly's party Friday?" wheezed Jackie, a little out of breath from her dash down the school halls. Jackie never walked; she always took off like she'd seen the biggest, hairiest spider that ever crawled.

"*Everybody's* going! Susan, Andy, and . . ." Jackie chattered on. *Everyone* who was *anyone* she meant. There were about ten kids in Carol's and Jackie's group who hung out together.

"Are you going, Jack?" Carol asked quietly.

"You bet! It's gonna be a great bash."

"Well, if you're going, I guess I'll go," Carol said slowly.

"Great! See you later!" Jackie called and tore down the hall.

Carol bumped into Cyndi on the way to her bicycle. "Want to grab a Coke, Carol?" Cyndi asked, flipping her blonde hair back. "I'm meeting the others there."

"I guess I'll go, if you're going," Carol hesitated.

Cyndi drawled, rather exasperatedly, "Well, come on, let's get going. We're already late."

All the girls knew Carol couldn't make up her mind about anything. Whether it was choosing a movie or where to eat (she couldn't even pick from the menu without seeing what her friends chose first!), or even what to wear. That was just Carol. It always had been and probably always would be. Her friends had gotten used to it.

Wishy-Washy People

How many people do you know who are like Carol? People who can't make up their minds are usually insecure—they so want to be a part of a group that they're afraid of making a different decision than everyone else. Fitting into a particular group is more important than being who they really are.

Carol had a hard time standing up for anything. She was a major pushover, and everyone knew it. But there's more about Carol. The sad thing is, she can't even stand up for what she believes in. Things like dating standards and religion. Whether she acts like a Christian or not depends on who she's with.

Stand-Up Power

The Bible says this about wishy-washy people: "That man (the man with divided allegiance) should not think he will receive anything from the Lord; he is a double-minded man, unstable in all he does" (James 1:7-8). And Revelation 3:15-16: "I know your deeds, that you are neither cold nor hot; I wish you were either one or the other! So, because you are lukewarm—neither hot nor cold—I am about to spit you out of my mouth."

God wants us to learn to take a stand, whether it's easy or not. Making decisions is part of the growing-up process. You wouldn't want to stay a baby forever, right?

Firm Ground

If you have a hard time making up your mind on things, remember what Paul says in Philippians:

> And this is my prayer: that your love may abound more and more in knowledge and depth of insight, so that you may be able to discern what is best and may be pure and blameless until the day of Christ . . . then you make my joy complete by being like-minded, having the same love, being one in spirit and purpose. Philippians 1:9-10; 2:2

Copy the verse into your school notebook so you'll always have it when you need it. In your prayer time today, ask God to help you stand firm.

26

Guys & Gals:
A Great Combo

☐ DAY ONE

Friends & Veggies: They're Good for You

1 0:00 P.M. Whew! Carmen was so relieved. Evan had been working on Carmen's stereo system for at least three hours. Some wires had shorted-out, and, as always, Evan was available. *Mr. Handyman* he called himself and that's what he was. He could fix anything—cars, stereos, blowdryers, you name it. He even helped Carmen's parents fix their bathroom faucet when it constantly drip-dripped.

"Evan, you're such a great guy. I can't believe I'm so lucky!" Carmen exclaimed.

"I know!" Evan grinned his cocky smirk and plopped back into the lambswool beanbag. Carmen could always count on him for a good laugh (or a good cry, whichever she needed).

Evan and Carmen had been good friends for over two years. He could always tell if she was upset about something and knew just how to draw her out. After all, who could resist that crazy, fun-loving, sensitive guy? He always put her in a better mood. Even Carmen's parents loved him because he was so comfortable, like an old pair of tennis shoes.

Carmen and Evan could talk about anything. It was cool how they could share things from different perspectives, without feeling threatened—or trying to impress each other—because they weren't dating. They were just solid-as-a-rock friends.

Top Teamwork

How many times have you heard, "Eat your vegetables. They're good for you!" since you were a toddler? Probably too many times to count. But it's true—veggies *are* good for you; they give your body some of the essential vitamins it needs to grow and be strong. Vitamins and your body make a dynamite team.

Friendships with the opposite sex can be wonderful and healthy, like eating veggies. Carmen's and Evan's is just one example. But all too often, it seems that the only guy/girl relationships are dating ones. Guys and girls could learn a lot from each other that would help in future relationships—things like how each sex acts, thinks, and reacts differently.

Research statistics show that one of the top qualities listed by couples with loving, lasting marriages is friendship. The couples knew each other as friends *before* they started dating. In some cases, they didn't even think of dating each other until several years later when it finally clicked.

Without the commitment of friends, you can be very lonely. Make it a goal to find kids of both sexes with whom you can be friends.

A Common Goal

The Bible gives a wonderful example of a man and woman who supported each other—Deborah and Barak. In fact, they were so necessary to each other that Barak wouldn't go into battle without Deborah (you can read their story in Judges chapters four and five). Imagine that! And especially in a time when women's roles were vastly different than they are today.

Proverbs 27:17 says,

> *As iron sharpens iron,*
> *so one man sharpens another.*

And Ecclesiastes 4:9 says,

> *Two are better than one,*
> *because they have a good return*
> *for their work.*

Friends are like that—they make us into better people, stretch our minds, and encourage our gifts.

One-a-Day Vitamins

Good friends of the opposite sex are like vitamins—necessary to your health. If you are a guy, do you have girl friends or girlfriends? If you are a girl, do you have boy friends or boyfriends? What do you think the difference is?

_____

_____

How do you treat the opposite sex? Is there someone of the opposite sex you'd like to be closer friends with (not as a date!)?

_____

_____

If you are lonely, ask Jesus to send you kids of both sexes with whom you can be friends.

☐ DAY TWO

We're Just Friends—
Honest

"**Y**ou and Marie are such a cute couple," Stephanie whispered.

Dave grimaced. Stephanie *would* have to pipe up during his favorite part of the movie. She was just like that. He hoped Marie didn't hear her.

Everyone thought he and Marie were a hot item—except him and Marie! They were very good friends, but *just friends*. Why couldn't anyone understand that? They'd been friends for seven years, even at the age when guys and girls weren't supposed to like being friends. They drove together to band practice and football games in Dave's rattly Chevy and ate lunch together.

They loved each other—as friends. And they felt so comfortable together—except when people kept nagging them.

Dave groaned. *Why did everyone make such a big deal out of him and Marie?* It was downright embarrassing.

"Steph, we're not a couple. We're just friends," Dave responded.

"Yeah, sure. So how come you're always together?" Stephanie demanded.

No one will ever understand. Dave sighed. *Only Marie and me.* He gave up trying to explain to Steph and just pointed out, "You're missing the best part of the movie!" Then he leaned back in his chair, exasperated.

Missing the Boat

A lot of guys and girls have great relationships just as friends—like Dave and Marie. Maybe you do. And you've been put in a position very much like them, and you hate it. You feel like it's ruining your friendship. You want to clobber the people who keep bugging you because they are totally missing the boat on this one.

What's Underneath

Have you ever wondered why some kids tease others? Maybe they are just downright rotten kids, and they love to give you a hard time. Or maybe it's because deep down they know they don't have good friends, and they are jealous. Or maybe they've never known or experienced a close friendship with a member of the opposite sex and just can't understand. They could be feeling lonely, wishing they had a friend like yours.

Understanding Motives

Maybe you're in the position of Dave and Marie. Or maybe you're Stephanie. Whichever you are, put yourself in their jeans. Make a list of how they could be feeling here:

_____

_____

The Bible says a lot about enduring things with patience—even pesky people:

> *We want each of you to show some diligence to the very end . . . We do not want you to become lazy, but to imitate those who through faith and patience inherit what has been promised . . . we who have fled to take hold of the hope offered to us may be greatly encouraged. We have this hope as an anchor for the soul, firm and secure.* Hebrews 6:11a-12, 18b-19a

No matter where you are, you can always escape—to God. He gives us a wall of refuge that no one can penetrate. Take time to thank him for that today. Ask him to remind you of those verses the next time you get exasperated with a situation.

☐ DAY THREE

I've Got
Warm Fuzzies

Remember Evan and Carmen from Day One? Well, there's more to their story.

As Evan and Carmen spent more time together, Carmen started realizing that Evan was really more than a friend for her.

I've got incredible warm fuzzies every time he's around, Carmen thought. *But I'm so scared. What if he doesn't feel the same way?*

They had both talked a lot about friendship the last year and how neither one of them really wanted to date anyone. They were just happy with who they were and neither wanted to get involved in a serious relationship—with anyone.

I don't want to lose his friendship, Carmen moaned, burying her face in her Mickey Mouse pillow. *What if I'm way off? Maybe he'll dump me.*

Carmen knew Evan enough to know that he didn't like leechy girls. When girls got too close, Evan backed off.

What a mess! Carmen sighed. She hoped that Evan wouldn't come over tonight. She didn't want to see him until she had her head straightened out again.

What Do I Do Now?

Carmen was in a mess. And she'd put herself there. What she didn't know was that Evan felt the same way. And he was as scared as she was—he didn't want to lose a friend either. What if it didn't work out? Could they go back to being just friends? Or would their relationship be ruined forever? It was a big gamble.

What's Love Anyway?

How many times do you hear someone say, "I think I'm in love!!"? Probably at least three times a day at school. Everyone has crushes and what others might call "puppy love," but real love? Is there such a thing?

Here's what the Bible says about it:

Love is patient, love is kind. It does not envy, it does not boast, it is not proud. It is not rude, it is not self-seeking, it is not easily angered, it keeps no record of wrongs. Love does not delight in evil but rejoices with the truth. It always protects, always trusts, always hopes, always perseveres. Love never fails.
1 Corinthians 13:4-8a

Doublecheck

If you think you're in love, doublecheck how you feel with the Scripture passage above. Do you really love that particular person, or are you in love with "being in love?" Do you sincerely love *that* particular person, or do you just want *A* person? Do you love that person as he or she is, or are you planning on changing him/her? Make some notes.

_____

_____

If you are "in love," tape the above verses right next to the phone. Read them every time before you call that person. Constantly remind yourself that 1 Corinthians 13 is the best kind of love—God's.

☐ DAY FOUR

I Only Have Eyes for You

Rick and Robin had dated for about six months. At first, they just went out together on Saturday nights for pizza or Cokes. But within the first month, it had begun to be every night. Then it got heavy. Robin just died if she didn't see Rick before school, at lunch, after school, and in the evening. She even left mushy love notes in his locker between classes.

Char was worried. This was getting pretty serious. She liked Rick a lot, and Robin was her best friend, but she felt left out. Robin and Rick were exclusive.

One Friday night when she and Robin were leaving together for a movie, Rick called. She heard Robin say, "No, I'm not doing anything. Be right over." As Char trudged home through the snow, she felt left in the cold once again. And that wasn't the only time. It became a ritual. She'd ask Robin to do something but then Rick would call up.

Char wanted to toss Robin right into the trash.

Exclusiveness

Char wasn't the only one who wanted to give up on Robin and Rick. Rick's guy friends felt the same way. But they weren't as persistent as Char. They just gave up and wrote him off as a lost cause.

Getting the brush off because "I'm-too-starry-eyed-over-my-boyfriend" is a real-life bummer. It hurts you, way down deep. But have you ever thought of something else? Not only does it hurt *you*, it hurts *them*.

Does every couple who dates stay together through all of high school? Or all of life? Certainly not. Robin was already on her third "serious" boyfriend, and she was only a sophomore!

If a couple who is dating breaks up, what happens? They really need their friends. But if they have constantly dumped their friends to spend time with their boyfriend/girlfriend, they could be in big trouble. People may not want to be around them anymore.

The Choice Is Ours

Only two people—Adam and Eve—could afford to be exclusive. They were the first created humans on earth, and they had the whole garden to themselves. But we don't. We are constantly surrounded by people who need us and our friendship. Today we can't be an Adam and Eve. Our world is not like that. (And besides, you'd be pretty embarrassed running around in just fig leaves on a date!)

Banana Splits or Skins?

If you're interested in another guy or girl, how do you treat your friends around your "flame"? Do you treat them as special and wonderful—like going out for banana splits—or like Robin did Char (like old banana skins?)

Jesus talked about the way that we should treat others:

> *So in everything, do to others what you would have them do to you, for this sums up the Law and the Prophets.* Matthew 7:12

If you are dating someone, write down how you treat your other friends. If you aren't dating anyone at this time, write down how you feel around one of your friends who *is* dating.

_____

_____

Ask God to make you more aware of the feelings of others around you.

☐ DAY FIVE

How Close Is Too Close?

enny and Alan had met in sixth grade at their church. But it wasn't until their junior year of high school that they had really noticed each other. Alan thought Jenny was one of the cutest girls he'd ever seen, so he asked her out. On their first date, they discovered they both loved carnivals and roller-coasters that gave you a sickening thud in your stomach.

They had such a blast together that they decided to go out again—on Friday. Jenny would never forget that night—she couldn't believe a kiss could be so great and could turn you to marshmallow inside. So they kissed again. And again. And then suddenly they were rolling around on Alan's couch (his parents were gone for the evening), and clothes were everywhere.

It had happened so fast. Jenny woke up the next morning, her head whirling. *How could I let that happen? But it felt so good I didn't want to stop.* Jenny felt incredibly guilty. She wondered how Alan felt. After all, they were both Christians and really involved in their youth group. Jenny hoped it wouldn't ruin their friendship, but somehow she felt that it already had.

No Fooling

Fooling around has consequences. Jenny was right. It had ruined a friendship that was just beginning to flourish. Alan steered clear of her at youth group for over five months, and then he started to date someone else. They had both lost their trust and respect for each other.

We've all heard the consequences of sex before marriage— the possibility of getting AIDS, herpes, and related diseases, or getting pregnant. Sure, that's enough to scare us, but is it enough to stop us from getting sexually involved outside of marriage?

God's Plan

In 1 Corinthians 6:18-20, God commands us to keep our bodies holy and pure:

> *Flee from sexual immorality. All other sins a man commits are outside his body, but he who sins sexually sins against his own body. Do you not know that your body is a temple of the Holy Spirit, who is in you, whom you have received from God? You are not your own; you were bought at a price. Therefore honor God with your body.*

God doesn't tell us that because he wants to be a cosmic killjoy. He does it because he loves us and wants to protect us. For he knows that when our bodies get involved, so do our minds. It's much harder to break off a relationship that isn't a good thing if you've been sexually involved with each other. Because no matter what happens in the relationship (and many times relationships based on sex fall apart within a few months because the guy and girl can't communicate except through sex), a part of you will still stay with that guy or girl.

God wants your marriage bed to be undefiled, so that just you and your husband or wife are in bed together. If you have had premarital sex with one or more girls or guys, you will be haunted by sexual ghosts when you make love with your spouse. Given the choice, wouldn't you pick a committed-for-a-lifetime love over a series of short flings?

There's Hope

If you have been involved in premarital sex, don't despair. There is hope for you. If you are truly sorry for what you have done, then ask God for his forgiveness. He gives it with open arms. "If we confess our sins, he is faithful and just and will forgive us our sins and purify us from all unrighteousness" (1 John 1:9).

But you must also take action. If you are still in the sexual relationship, then you must take steps so that it doesn't happen again. Avoid being alone with the other person, especially in places where it would be easy to slip into old patterns, or break totally away from the person. (Most couples discover that without the sex, they don't have much in common anymore.)

Whether you are in this situation right now or not, you could be in the near future. Write down your guidelines for dating here. Then stick to them no matter what.

_____

_____

_____

If your friends who have had sex are telling you how great it is, or are teasing you about being a virgin, remember one very important thing: You can become like them any day, but they can *never* be like you.

If you or a friend are in this situation now, claim the power of Christ in 1 Corinthians 10:13:

> *No temptation has seized you except what is common to man. And God is faithful; he will not let you be tempted beyond what you can bear. But when you are tempted, he will also provide a way out so that you can stand up under it.*

Cliques & Clones Will Break My Bones

☐ DAY ONE

Who Put These Price Tags On Anyway?

J ulius slammed the padlock on his athletic locker. *I'm such a clod!* he thought. *How come I have to be so uncoordinated?* He picked at the worn leather on his football. He felt pretty lucky just to make it on the junior varsity team this year.

Julius felt like he was constantly messing up. And that everyone saw him trip over his size 13 feet at least once a day. Like a giant Labrador, he galloped through the school halls. He never could get his arms and legs to go in the same direction at the same time. And besides that, he had braces—a full set of gleaming metal, just like Jaws in the James Bond movies.

I wish I were like Ron. He always has it together. Man, he's even got muscles in all the right places!

Julius kicked his locker for the third time that day.

"I Wish" Syndrome

Have you ever wished you looked like someone else? Or even *were* someone else? Maybe you've battled with the pudges your whole life—you look at a Hershey's bar, and it melts right onto your hips—or, even worse, onto your face. Maybe you are a senior, but you only weigh 89 pounds. The only position you could play on the football team is the football. Or maybe your parents are divorced, and you wish you had perfect parents like your friends.

One-of-a-Kind

There are lots of reasons why you could wish you were someone else. But you know what? God created you uniquely you.

> Before I formed you in
>   the womb I knew you,
> Before you were born
>   I set you apart. Jeremiah 1:5a

God knew you even while you were being created! And he made you as you are—a redhead, an athlete, a good cook, whatever! He gave you naturally wavy hair or straight-as-a-stick hair. And by putting together millions of variations, he made you—and there's no one else *exactly* like you in the whole world!

God values your uniqueness. And because he has created you as you are, he expects you to use what he has given you. Maybe you aren't the greatest athlete in the world, but you can bake up a storm. Then bake brownies for someone who is down. Maybe you are not a mechanical genius on cars like your buddy, but you are great with math. Then tutor someone who is really struggling.

Don't slip into the common trap of determining your self-worth by outward things like grades or good looks. We are created in the image of God (see Ephesians 2:10)—so we already have worth! Like Julius, we need to learn to take our eyes off ourselves, off "How do *I* look? How am *I* doing?" and put them on helping someone else.

Through Your Own Eyes

Cut a big heart out of paper. Then fold it in half vertically. On the left side, list three things that you like about yourself (it could be personality, appearance, something you're good at). On the right side, write: "I am created in the image of God."

How can you use what you've just listed to help someone out?

_____

_____

The next time you wish you were someone else, refer back to your personal valentine. Thank God that he made you uniquely you!

☐ DAY TWO

Steamy Situations

Maria scooted farther over toward the window. She couldn't believe that she had let herself get into this. Here she was—at Romantic Ridge—with José.

Maria had been so excited when José asked her out on Friday night for a doubledate with Marcy and Greg. The movie had been great fun. But then, just as they were on their way to Pizza Hut, Marcy had said, "Hey, guys, let's make a detour for a few minutes."

When Maria agreed to the detour, she didn't know they'd end up at Romantic Ridge. But here they were. Marcy and Greg were kissing up a storm in the front seat. Maria felt pretty uncomfortable sitting in the back seat. She hoped no one would recognize her.

Firm Like a Rock

If you were Maria, what would you do? Crawl under the car seat? Maria is really in a hard position. She doesn't want to be "chicken," but she knows that people who park at Romantic Ridge don't have good reputations either. She doesn't want to be like them.

Peer pressure is tough. You face it every day. And even though it's common, it doesn't make it easier! You must make decisions about what kind of clothes you're going to wear, where you are going to go with your friends, what crowd you're going to hang around with, and what kind of a date you want to be.

You're Not the Only One

You're not the only one who had to face tough decisions about dating practices. Joseph did too! He was in his 20's, at the height of his sexual drive, when Potiphar's wife, an older lady, went after him. Her persuasion wasn't subtle either: Basically she dived for him and tried to drag him into her bed (Genesis 39:12). And the poor guy had to flee from her without his coat!

Maybe someone isn't trying to "make out" or "go all the way" with you, but you still have hard choices to make about all kinds of temptation—sexual or otherwise.

Joseph knew what to do with temptation. He ran away from it because he knew God wouldn't be pleased if he gave in.

When the Pressure's On

James encourages us to take a stand when things seem tough:

> *Consider it pure joy, my brothers, when you face trials of many kinds, because you know that the testing of your faith develops perseverance. Perseverance must finish its work so that you may be mature and complete, not lacking anything. Blessed is the man who perseveres under trial, because when he has stood the test, he will receive the crown of life that God has promised to those who love him.* James 1:2-4, 12

Even though the consequences of obeying God weren't easy (Joseph was thrown in prison because he was falsely accused of attempted rape), God honored him—he became the top leader over the land of Egypt and had all the wealth and power he could have ever imagined! God will also honor you for standing up for him: maybe not through riches or power, but through a good reputation, among other things.

When have you faced a peer-pressure decision? What did you do then? What would you do now?

_____

_____

God can give you the power to resist any temptation. Ask him for it.

☐ DAY THREE

Who's Your Hero?

JD. and Sonya bounced up and down in their seats. They couldn't wait for the concert to start. After saving up for the tickets, they knew it would be worth it. And they'd even talked Mom and Dad into letting them go—a major miracle.

Ten minutes 'til eight o'clock. Soon she'd come on. They couldn't believe they were actually going to get to see her after listening to her records for two years. And this year she'd been in the top ten almost every week.

The concert was pretty good, but not what they expected. She only sang two of her hit songs, and the rest must have been old stuff they didn't know. J.D.'s and Sonya's steps slowed as they walked home. They were both disappointed—maybe she wasn't all they'd built her up to be.

Hero Worship

All of us have heroes. When we were little, it might have been our father or mother, or the ice cream man who drove the truck with the jingly bells. Maybe now it's a rock star or a movie star. It could be your favorite macho lawyer on TV or the girl on the commercials with the perfect body.

But whoever your hero is, you need to stand him or her up to this passage of Scripture:

Be imitators of God, therefore, as dearly loved children and live a life of love . . . there must not be even a hint of sexual immorality, or of any kind of impurity, or of greed . . . Nor should there be obscenity, foolish talk or coarse joking, which are out of place, but rather thanksgiving . . . Let no one deceive you with empty words. . . . For you were once darkness, but now you are light in the Lord . . . Be very careful, then, how you live—not as unwise but as wise, making the most of every opportunity, because the days are evil. Ephesians 5:1-16

Not All They're Cracked Up to Be

Human heroes usually aren't all we think they are. And sometimes we're disappointed—like J.D. and Sonya were. When that happens, the hero takes a rather nasty fall off of your pedestal. Usually it's pretty hard for him to get back on. Even if he does manage it, now you see the cracks where you had to glue him back together.

Maybe this has happened in your own family—Dad, who you thought was perfect, has been having an affair. Or Mom, the always happy and stable lady, had to take off a month because of mental depression. Or maybe you discovered that your older brother whom you adore is gay. You're all confused.

There is only one real hero. This hero never falls off his pedestal because he can't sin—it's not a part of his nature. He is always perfect, something hard for us to imagine. Who's the Real Hero? Jesus Christ, the only one who will never fail or disappoint us. And even better, he's approachable—at any time, at all times. You don't even have to buy tickets to see him!

On the Pedestal

List two people who influence your decisions the most. In light of God's standards in Ephesians 5, are they a positive or negative influence on you? Give specifics.

_____

_____

Ask God to give you his kind of wisdom about whom you put on your pedestal.

☐ DAY FOUR

The Lone Ranger

J ack the Jock strutted down the hall of Lincoln High. His classmates turned from their chatter to watch him.

Last night, as usual, he had wowed them all at the soccer game by scoring a hat-trick (three goals) in a really tough game against Westmont. The guy was incredible—*Super Jock* they called him. He was good at anything and everything athletic and was even captain of the varsity baseball team (as a junior!).

He was such a together guy—super efficient. He did everything well, and what's more, he did it by himself. His grades topped the chart. And because he was such an awesome guy, the other kids didn't even get mad when he wrecked the curve. But somehow, Jack stayed away from all the rest of the kids. It wasn't that Jack was mean or sulky or anything like that, he just didn't hang around with them. They couldn't figure out why. Then after awhile, they convinced themselves, "Well, he doesn't need us anyway. He's got everything he needs."

Meanwhile, Jack padded down the halls to class alone.

On the Outside

On the outside, Jack seemed totally independent. But what was he like on the inside?

What nobody knew was that Jack stayed aloof on purpose.

NO ARTIFICIAL FLAVORS   100% Friendship ·

He wanted friends, but he was scared for anyone to get to know him too well. Because his dad had divorced his mom, he felt he had to be the man of the house now. Two years after the divorce, his mom still acted like a basket case and threatened to kill herself when she got depressed. And what's worse, both of his parents were supposed to be Christians.

At the Heart

All of us know someone who is a loner. Usually we label them in categories: "She's a band fag," "He's a nerd," "She's super radical," "He's a jock," because then we can box them up neatly. It's easy to attach stereotypes to someone because of their age, social rank, or sex. How many times have you heard generalizations like: "All teenagers are irresponsible!" "Dumb blonde!" "Teenage Drivers!"?

Jesus had some stern words for those who judge others:

> *"Do not judge, or you too will be judged. For in the same way you judge others, you will be judged, and with the measure you use, it will be measured to you."* Matthew 7:1-2

In other words, if you name-call and categorize other people, the same thing will happen to you.

In Their Shoes

Who is the lone ranger in your school? Put yourself in his or her shoes for a minute. How do you think he or she really feels?

_____

_____

Write down one thing that you can do for this person this week and then do it, knowing that God is smiling down on you. Ask a parent, youth leader, or a close friend to keep you accountable.

_____

☐ DAY FIVE

The Right Kind of Nit-picky

L inda's mind churned. She was in a real pickle. Finally the "cool" kids had invited her to go out with them Friday night. But there was a big problem—they were going to a park that was way out in the country, a place known for wild parties. She wanted to do something with them because they seemed like they had a lot of fun together. But still she was uncomfortable. She knew her parents wouldn't approve. So she told them no. Raising their eyebrows, they said, "Hey, baby, it's your loss."

But the next Monday she knew different. Shock waves skittered across the school. Everyone knew by noon hour about the terrible accident. Three of the kids who talked to her were dead. The driver had been drunk, and they found beer in the car.

The car I would have been riding in, Linda thought. Her stomach turned for the rest of the day.

Life Is a Cafeteria

Life is like going through a cafeteria line—we pick and choose the things that look good to us. One day of bad choices in food might not kill us (unless we get the stuff they *call* pizza), but one bad choice of a friend might. It won't necessarily kill us in body, like it could have killed Linda, but it could kill us in spirit. If you choose friends who are always depressed, you could become a real bum-

mer to be around. If you choose sarcastic friends, you might de-
velop a sharp-edged tongue.

Picking and Reaping

What kind of friends do you have? The Bible says that you should
pick your friends carefully because you will become like them.
In Proverbs, wise Solomon says,

> *He who walks with the wise*
> *   grows wise,*
> *But a companion of fools*
> *   suffers harm.* (13:20)

Maybe the friends you have right now won't be yours for life, but
the *type* of friends you choose will set a pattern for the rest of your
life.

Hanging Out Together

Write down the names of two of your closest friends. Also write
down what kind of reputations they have.

Friend   *Reputation*

_____

_____

According to Proverbs 27:19 and 13:20, are any of these relationships harmful? What are you going to do about those that are?

_____

_____

Remember that the friends you choose affect who you become
down the road. If God were standing next to you now, would he
be pleased with the friends you hang out with? Why or why not?

_____

Rocks in My Reeboks

☐ DAY ONE

Who's Better?

T hursday night, midnight—the end of the semester. Andy got up from his chair, stretched, and yawned. It was high-pressure time for Andy. His brain felt like cottage cheese.

The next morning his best friend Mark roared over in his Jeep to pick him up. "You're the best!" Andy yelled and grinned at Mark, stretched out in his old four-wheeler.

"Yeah, I know, old man," Mark replied. "Hey, did you study for old Laver's test?"

"A lot. I gotta do well on it, or I won't get into Edison next year." Andy sighed.

"Are you kidding?" Mark exploded. "I didn't even review the stuff. It'll be a cinch!" Andy couldn't believe it. Of course, Mark was a real brain and all, but not study?

The test was tough, a real hair-twister. Andy got a C–. Guess what Mark got? An A! He aced it. Andy felt sick. It was the old I'm-not-as-smart-as-him-but-I-wish-I-were problem. Why did he have to work so much harder than Mark just to pass? Suddenly, Andy felt a cold stab of jealousy.

Pass or Fail?

There's always someone who's better than you. If you're the smartest kid in your school, then the kid from your rival school is smarter. Or maybe you're a whiz at math but impossibly dumb at

English literature. Maybe you're a klutz and wish you were like Joe Athletic. No matter who you are or what age you are or where you live, someone will always be better than you.

An Old Problem

Saul, in the Old Testament, had the same problem. He was a great king, with all the wealth and position you could ever want. But guess who he was jealous of? A shepherd/servant boy named David, who went into battle and fought *for* Saul.

Then it got even worse. When David marched back from battle, the people sang, "Saul killed his thousands but David his ten thousands." David killed at least ten times as many people as Saul. And because of jealousy, Saul tried to kill David. Why? You see, on their test, David got an A and Saul only a C–.

You're the One Who Counts

Even though James lived a long time ago, he hits the nail on the head when he talks about jealousy:

> *For where you have envy and selfish ambition, there you find disorder and every evil practice. But the wisdom that comes from heaven is first of all pure; then peace-loving, considerate, submissive, full of mercy and good fruit, impartial and sincere. Peacemakers who sow in peace raise a harvest of righteousness.* James 3:16-18

It doesn't matter how well you do compared to someone else. What does count is what you do and think in relation to yourself. If you try your hardest and have a good attitude no matter what you do, then you have passed the test with flying colors.

Name one person you are jealous of (whether it's because of clothes, money, social status, beauty, whatever). Also write down why you feel jealous.

_____

_____

The next time you see that person, remind yourself that God loves you—just the way you are. Keep telling yourself every time you feel twinged by jealousy.

☐ DAY TWO

Hey, Did You Hear About . . . ?

Jim and Eliot were "Soul-bro's." At least Jim thought so. Then one day Jim overheard Eliot telling something personal about him in the locker room. Two weeks ago Jim had finally gotten up enough guts to ask Rachel out. She was a really sweet girl, and Jim liked her a lot.

The way Eliot told the story, it sounded like Jim and Rachel had made out in the back seat. Jim was disgusted—and steaming! It wasn't even true. Of course, he knew that Eliot loved to add color and details to stories, but he never thought Eliot would ever do something like that to him.

Standing there in his underwear, Jim felt more than naked. Eliot had betrayed him. He wondered what he should do about it.

Jim didn't have to wonder long. By the afternoon, the whole school knew all the facts—what they thought were facts anyway. Old Broadcast Mouth Brenda, who had a megaphone for a voice, had done her job on the gossip hotline well.

The Gossip Hotline

Is all really fair in friendship and war? Or are there rules? Sometimes we wonder—especially when someone betrays us. The gossip hotline is not only news—it's *bad* news. The Bible has a lot to say about it (see Proverbs 26:17-28 for some colorful examples of how God feels about gossips).

More to the Story

Samson was a guy who really felt betrayed. You see, he met this girl Delilah—the #1 two-faced woman. Delilah was gorgeous, a real babe. Every guy was drooling over her. Well, Delilah took special interest in Samson, who was also a good-looking hunk of a guy, and he *really* liked her. A tough guy, Samson had only one weakness—pretty women. And Delilah knew it.

But there is more to the story. Actually Delilah was just pretending to like Samson so she could get a secret out of him, the secret of his strength. Her persistence won, and she got what she wanted. Then she told the people who had hired her.

What was the result? Samson's long hair was chopped off, his eyes were blinded, and he was chained and tossed into prison. Eventually a building fell on him and crushed him to death.

Most likely none of you will go through what Samson did. But sometimes you might feel like a building fell splat! right on you. You can't believe someone has betrayed you—especially if you thought he was your friend.

One of the most powerful tools we have is the human tongue. Even though the tongue is a small part of the human body, it is extremely hard to tame (see James 3:8). What comes out of our mouth can be one of two things—encouraging, or destroying. Paul gives us some guidelines:

> *Do not let any unwholesome talk come out of your mouths, but only what is helpful for building others up according to their needs, that it may benefit those who listen.* Ephesians 4:29

Taming the Tongue

When Old Broadcast Mouth Brenda tells you some sizzling news about someone in school, think three things before you pass it on: *Is it true?; Is it kind?; Does it have to be said?*

Think of a situation where you or someone else was betrayed. How did you feel then? Now? What did you do about it? What do you think Christ would have done about it?

_____

_____

The next time you hear gossip, walk in Christ's sandals.

☐ DAY THREE

Candy in My Locker

Math brain! Nerd! Ryan could tell that's what they were thinking as he walked down the hall toward his calculus room. Sure, he looked the part with his glasses, calculator, and stack of notebooks and textbooks. He couldn't help being a math genius. Neither could his dad—it ran in the family.

Today he'd been surprised to find his favorite, a Snickers, taped to his door with a note that said, "From an admirer." *Wow!* he thought. The rest of the day he whizzed around the school, humming to himself. The next day he found another chocolate bar—he couldn't believe his luck! On Thursday morning there was a big Hershey's kiss tied with a bow. Now he knew someone was in love with him.

Then he found out who it was. Carleen—a really popular girl who was super dumb in math. She walked up to him and said, "Hey, how'd you like your notes? I wanted to see if you could come over to my house tonight."

"Sure," Ryan grinned. "Meet you after school?" That night Carleen dripped sugar all over him. He helped her finish her math assignment and then gave her tips on what to study for the test.

Friday's math test was hard. After it was all over, Ryan walked up to Carleen and asked, "Hey, how'd you do?"

"Great with all your help!" she replied. But somehow, by looking at her and seeing the little sweet-as-sour-grapes smirk she gave her friends, Ryan's heart sank. He felt used.

People Aren't Things

All of us have felt used at some time in our lives. And we've probably done it to someone else ourselves! Somehow we get things mixed up: instead of using things and loving people, we love things and use people.

Catching the Hypocrite

God protects human dignity. He encourages us to be truthful:

> *Put off your old self, which is being corrupted by its deceitful desires . . . Therefore each of you must put off falsehood and speak truthfully to his neighbor, for we are all members of one body.* Ephesians 4:22b, 25

Carleen was a hypocrite—someone who pretended to be and do one thing, but actually was and did another. She led poor Ryan to believe she was interested in him just to get a good grade on a math test. Then she dropped him kerplunk! And to make his humiliation worse, she did it in front of all her friends.

'Fessing Up

Complete the following sentences.

I wasn't really truthful when I _____

_____

Instead of caring about him/her, I had my own best interests in

mind when I _____

_____

You might want to pray the following prayer:

> Jesus, I'm sorry that I used _____. Please give me courage to apologize to _____, and remind me in the future that hypocrisy hurts both _____ and me. Help me to grow to be the kind of friend that you want me to be. Amen.

☐ DAY FOUR

Superiority
Scene

Best friend? Yeah, sure! Sandy muttered, as Allison bounced off with the other cheerleaders in her short blue and white skirt. It had happened again—just like she knew it would.

Sandy and Allison had been forever-best-friends at Franklin High. They'd been friends for so long that the other kids at school teased them about living in the same skin.

This year was different. Allison had made varsity cheerleader, and she was pretty excited. But life was all downhill into bumsville for Sandy. Allison looked really cute the first pep rally of the year in her outfit, flinging around her pompoms. Suddenly everyone wanted Allison around. No one seemed to notice Sandy, who felt like sinking right through the mint green walls. But that wasn't too bad—she still had Allison.

By November, though, Allison really didn't have time for Sandy anymore. Whenever they had made plans, Allison got a better offer, and off she'd go. She still *acted* like Sandy's best friend when she had time to be, but Allison didn't make much time for Sandy anymore. And when she did, she kept talking about what she did with all the other cheerleaders and football players and how cool it was to be part of the in-crowd.

She thinks I'm not good enough for her anymore! Sandy thought. Ooh—that hurt! *After all these years, how could she? Wasn't their friendship worth something?* Sandy felt like a worm squished on a sidewalk.

It's Your Choice

When Allison made the varsity squad and started meeting new people, she made a choice about how she'd treat Sandy and her other old friends. But Allison got caught up in the excitement of pep rallies and games and forgot to be sensitive to Sandy.

Joseph also experienced some new, unexpected privileges. First, he was his dad's favorite. And he, like Allison, wasn't very sensitive to his brothers. He strutted around in his special coat and bragged about strange dreams of superiority over them.

I'm Better than You

Later, after years of slavery and imprisonment, Joseph had another opportunity to lord it over his jealous brothers. This time he really *was* high and mighty (he had become Pharaoh's #1 assistant and governor of all Egypt), but he didn't act superior to his brothers. He never once said, "I'm better than you!" Instead he lovingly showed them that he considered them part of his "in-crowd," even after all the bad things they had done to him over the years.

Where Do You Fit in the Game?

Have you ever felt like someone was putting the superiority scene over on you? How did you react?

_____

_____

Remember that the Bible says:

> *Live in harmony with one another. Do not be proud, but be willing to associate with people of low position. Do not be conceited.* Romans 12:16

Is there someone you are lording it over? It could be a next-door neighbor kid who's pesky, a new teen at school, or a brother or sister. If so, you may want to pray: God, I'm really sorry that I've been lording it over _____ . Help me to remember how much hurt I'm causing by acting superior. And help me to learn how to love in the way you would. Amen.

☐ DAY FIVE

The Big Letdown

K evin was sweating it out. The history final was tough—he basically had to write a survey of everything he had learned that semester. Whew!

He looked over at his friend T.J., grinned, and gave him the thumbs up sign. Studying hard was paying off; he knew this stuff like his Nike shoes label. But T.J. looked panic-stricken.

Kevin concentrated on his test. Just as he was two-thirds through, he felt someone's eyes on him. It was T.J. He had scooted his desk over a bit, and he was eye-balling Kevin's answers.

Kevin couldn't believe it! His buddy T.J. was cheating—and off *his* test. Moving his arm closer to his test, Kevin blocked T.J.'s view. But then he saw T.J. mouth wordlessly, *Come on, man!* Uncovering his test, Kevin started writing again. But his heart was heavy; he didn't even want to be T.J.'s friend anymore.

Not Perfect

Maybe, like Kevin, you've discovered that people aren't perfect. Kevin couldn't believe T.J. would cheat, especially when they were both Christians. But even Christians aren't perfect. God calls us to be the light of the world (Matthew 5:14), but sometimes our lights flicker. As we try to become more like Christ, we realize what a long road it is by ourselves. But if we claim his power, we have more than enough for victory.

Classic Examples

The disciples—a perfect group, right? Look again. Peter was an impetuous, loud-mouthed fisherman who denied Christ when things got too hot for him; Thomas questioned everything; John was a hot-head; Judas wanted to change the world with a revolution, and then when things didn't go his way, he betrayed his friends and later killed himself. The disciples were only too human, yet God used them to make big steps toward his kingdom.
Paul described the goal of our lives this way:

> Not that I have already obtained all this, or have already been made perfect, but I press on to take hold of that for which Christ Jesus took hold of me. Brothers, I do not consider myself yet to have taken hold of it. But one thing I do: Forgetting what is behind and straining toward what is ahead, I press on toward the goal to win the prize for which God has called me heavenward in Christ Jesus. Philippians 3:12-14

Do you know who Paul was before he became Paul the apostle? He was Saul, the murderer of Christians. Yet God changed his life around so that he could be a witness for Christ.

Charging Your Battery

Maybe a friend has let you down. Or you've let yourself down by doing something that you wish you hadn't done. Write about it here (and then put your book in a safe, secret place):

_____

_____

There's hope for you. Just as God transformed the lives of some very unusual people, he can charge your life with his power.
On a piece of paper, draw a battery. (Don't worry, you don't have to be an artist!) Divide the battery in half. Label one side − and the other side +. On the − side, write "I am human." And on the + side, write: You, _____ (insert your name), are from God and have overcome them, because the one who is in you is greater than the one who is in the world. (1 John 4:4)
Which side do you think is stronger?

Nasty Little Papercuts

☐ DAY ONE

Enduring the "Dump"

Bianca and Corey were very-best-friends-in-the-whole-world. That summed them up well. Ever since they both moved here in fifth grade, they stuck together like superglue and fingers. Even their parents were best friends.

One day Bianca was walking down the hall when she spied Corey. "Hey, Cor! Want to get ice cream after school? Mom gave me some extra fun money!"

Shock set in when Corey retorted, "Ice cream? Are you kidding? That's kid stuff. I'm going out with Lisa and Annette for Cherry 7-Up floats at the Denmark." She stressed *the Denmark*, a fashionable place where only the highest-class kids hung out.

On the way home, Bianca's pace was much slower than usual. When she got to her room, she felt empty. Corey usually walked home with her.

The next day Bianca decided to forget it and just approach Corey as if nothing had happened. But she didn't have the chance. On her locker she found this note in Corey's scrawly writing:

Dear Bianca,
I really don't want to be friends with you anymore. We've been friends a long time, and I need a change. I know you'll understand.
                    Corey

With shaking hands, Bianca pushed the purple note paper into the back of her science textbook. Then she made her way to the restroom. She didn't even hear when the bell rang.

Tough Squeeze

Poor Bianca. She felt like David in the Psalms: "Even my close friend, whom I trusted, he who shared my bread, has lifted up his heel against me" (Psalm 41:9). Even though only one person had slam-dunked her, her world had caved in. Her heart felt like someone was squeezing all the blood out of it. *I just don't understand!* her heart cried.

On a Desert Island

Jesus knew what it was like to be deserted. Peter denied him three times and ran off to save his own hide. And to top it off, most of his friends deserted him when he was nailed to the cross.

Jesus understands when you feel you are on a desert island—and someone stole all the life boats.

Band-aids

David wrote some psalms while he was running in fear of his life. He felt deserted—and betrayed—by all those he loved. And yet he had a champion wound-wrapper.

> *The righteous cry out, and the LORD hears them;*
> *he delivers them from all their troubles.*
> *The LORD is close to the brokenhearted*
> *and saves those who are crushed in spirit.*
> *A righteous man may have many troubles,*
> *but the LORD delivers him from them all.* Psalm 34:17-19

In what areas do you feel wounded today?

_____

_____

If you are wearing someone's foot mark on your face, ask Jesus to give you new hope so that you can pick up and carry on.

☐ DAY TWO

The Great Blow-off

uys' Night Out! Whoopee! Ron high-slapped the door frame and raced out the door. He'd been waiting a long time for this. A month ago, he and Jeff had planned to do the night up big—together. Just the two of them.

At 6:00, as Ron was pulling on his Levi's, Jeff called. "Hey, bud! Would you mind if I brought Dan along tonight?"

Ron froze. "I thought you said it would be the two of us."

"Yeah, I know. But I already told Dan he could come along," Jeff replied.

Ron told him he guessed it was okay and hung up. Furious, he paced in front of the mirror. *Just great! I knew it wouldn't work out. Dan would have to come—tonight.*

That night at the movies, it was so packed they could find only two seats together. So Ron sat a few rows down. Afterwards they went out for tacos. Jeff and Dan were still talking about karate practice, and since Ron didn't know anything about karate, he kept his mouth shut. He felt like a pesky insect.

Mosquitoes Are Pests

At some time in our lives, all of us have felt like pests. Whether people are actually slapping at us or not, we feel that they are. It isn't easy to get hyped about something and then be disappointed either. Ron felt blown-off—like he wasn't important enough to be around. If Jeff and Dan weren't trying to ignore him, they had a strange way of showing it.

Revenge Is a Flyswatter

Getting back at them for being such snobs was the first thing on Ron's mind—a very human response. When we are hurt, we want revenge. We want to make someone else pay for hurting us. And it doesn't matter if "paying" is physical or emotional. The old saying, "Sticks and stones may break my bones but words can never hurt me" isn't true. Verbal pay-back is as hurtful as physical abuse. And it happens a lot in families, even Christian ones.

Paul warns us in Romans 12:17-21:

> *Do not repay anyone evil for evil. Be careful to do what is right in the eyes of everybody. If it is possible, as far as it depends on you, live at peace with everyone. Do not take revenge, my friends, but leave room for God's wrath, for it is written: "It is mine to avenge; I will repay," says the Lord. On the contrary: "If your enemy is hungry, feed him; if he is thirsty, give him something to drink. In doing this, you will heap burning coals on his head." Do not be overcome by evil, but overcome evil with good.*

That's enough to stop a flyswatter, don't you think?

Pest Control

When have you felt like a pesky insect? What did you do about it?

_____

_____

Have you ever treated anyone else like one? Think back.

_____

_____

Ask Christ to put his forgiveness in your heart toward the persons who have wronged you and understanding toward those you have wronged.

☐ DAY THREE

It Takes Guts . . . Bleecckk

Remember Ron, Jeff, and Dan? Well, Ron stayed angry for over a week at Jeff. After all, it was pretty mean of Jeff to ignore him all night and spend time with Dan (who wasn't supposed to be invited anyway).

Jeff acted pretty normal around Ron, and that made Ron even angrier. Finally, he'd had it with Jeff. Jeff had to know that he had hurt him. Ron decided to talk with him. The problem was getting him alone. A popular guy, Jeff always had crowds around him. Ron finally captured him after fifth period.

"Hey, man, I really need to talk with you about something," Ron hesitated.

"Sure! Do you want to grab the bench after school? I've got half an hour before I have to be at practice," Jeff gushed.

As soon as the end-of-the-day bell rang, Ron leaped out of his seat. This thing was bugging him, and he wanted it resolved.

Ron told Jeff how he had felt that night and was feeling now. Jeff was astounded. "I didn't know you felt like that, Ron! I just thought it would be nice to invite Dan since he was a new kid at school and all. I didn't know it would hurt your feelings."

After they talked, Ron felt limp and relieved. Jeff was really a nice guy after all!

A Fairy Tale Story

Maybe you're thinking to yourself, "That's a fairy-tale ending. No macho guy would admit to all that." Sure, not all endings to problems work out that easily, but we at least have to try. It *can* happen that way. Christ holds us responsible to live in harmony with all others because as Christians, we are to be role-models of him to others.

I Just Can't!

Maybe you're saying, "But I've really been hurt. You don't understand how I feel or you couldn't ask me to go to that jerk!" Maybe someone has backbitten you, told something they shouldn't have, or made up a lie about you. But Christ still holds us responsible to go to that person. He wants no division between his children. He wants us to be at peace in all our relationships and calls us to live out the words of 2 Corinthians 2:5-10a:

> If anyone has caused grief, he has not so much grieved me as he has grieved all of you, to some extent—not to put it too severely. The punishment inflicted on him by the majority is sufficient for him. Now instead, you ought to forgive and comfort him, so that he will not be overwhelmed by excessive sorrow. I urge you, therefore, to reaffirm your love for him. The reason I wrote to you was to see if you would stand the test and be obedient in everything. If you forgive anyone, I also forgive him.

If you feel or cause sorrow, Christ also feels it. And the rest of the body of Christ feels it, because we are all parts of one unified body.

I Can

Confronting someone takes a lot of guts. Whether we are the ones who've been hurt, or the ones who have done the hurting, God can give us the power to make the first step. Is there someone you should approach today? Write the name here.

_____

Write down some positive qualities about this person. When you talk with him or her, first list the good qualities you appreciate about the person. People are more willing to listen if you compliment them first before presenting the problem.

_____

_____

Christ says in Philippians 4:13: "I can do everything through him who gives me strength." Ask Christ to help you swallow your ego and to give you gutsy courage.

☐ DAY FOUR

When You Mess Up

Kathy sank into the blue leather couch. *I've made such a mess of things! And it's all my fault!* She knew no one else could get her out of what she had done. This one topped the charts.

Erika had only been at Churchill High for six weeks after moving there from California. As far as Kathy knew, she was an only child. Since Kathy and Erika both played flute in band, they hit it off immediately. After spending lots of time with Kathy, Erika had dropped a bombshell.

Erika and Kathy had been munching peanut butter cookies in the kitchen. Then Erika said, "Can I tell you something? Can you keep a secret?"

Kathy felt privileged that Erika wanted to tell her. "Sure," she said, without giving it a second thought.

"Well, there's something I've been wanting to tell you for a long time. You see, I do have a brother—back in California. He's nine years older than me, and—" her voice slowed to a whisper. "Well, he's gay, and he lives with another guy in an apartment." Kathy was shocked. Sure, she knew that some people were gay, but she never knew anyone whose *brother* was gay.

A couple weeks later at school, Kathy and some of her friends were talking. Somehow, they got on the subject of gay people. All of a sudden, before she realized it, Erika's secret had slipped out. It didn't take long to get around school. The kids teased Erika like crazy, and it wasn't long before she changed schools.

Kathy felt responsible. And she was.

When There's No Eraser

Kathy is stuck in an awful position. After ruining someone's life and reputation, there's not much she can do to repair it. It's just like poking someone's eye out; there's nothing you can do to make that eye grow back. Kathy can't erase that news from the minds or memories of all the kids at Churchill High. She is miserable.

White-Out

Kathy can't change the circumstances, but she does need to confess her sin: "If we confess our sins, he is faithful and just and will forgive us our sins and purify us from all unrighteousness" (1 John 1:9). Confessing our sins to God is like taking a bottle of white-out to them. They are gone forever from God's book. But we must do more than just confess our sin to God. Let's turn back to Kathy's situation.

Not only must Kathy confess her sin to God and say she is sorry, but she must take action. First she must admit to Erika that what she did was wrong, and that she's very sorry. Then she must ask Erika to forgive her. Finally she must forgive herself (which is perhaps the hardest of the three things to do). We'll talk more about these steps in the upcoming days.

Wiping Up the Mess

Kathy can't change what happened, but she can change her reaction to it. She can mope around and say, "I'm such a loser." Or she can get up and face the day, determining to live as a forgiven child of Jesus Christ.

What do you feel you have made a mess of lately?

_____

_____

If you have hurt someone else, don't let the week go by without contacting that person. If he or she won't talk with you, leave a special note and sneak it into his or her locker. Or bake something to show you care about the hurt.

Read David's psalm for encouragement today:

Praise the Lord, O my soul,
And forget not all his benefits—
Who forgives all your sins,
And heals all your diseases,
Who redeems your life from the pit
And crowns you with love and compassion. Psalm 103:2-4

☐ DAY FIVE

Healing the Wound— for Good

Again we meet Kathy and Erika. But this time, let's look at Erika's side.

Erika was pretty upset she had to transfer to a different school, but she was even more upset because of the reason. The kids were teasing her and asking her, "If your brother's gay, are you a lesbian?" Then they would skitter off down the hall, laughing.

Erika was crushed. How could Kathy tell anyone? Erika had trusted her with her deepest secret. When Kathy called four months later, she was still adjusting to her new school. At first Erika didn't even want to talk with Kathy. But she was so lonely she agreed to hear what Kathy had to say.

Kathy poured out her story in tears and said how sorry she was. Up till now, Erika had seen her as an enemy. Suddenly she seemed human—she hurt just like Erika.

But still Erika couldn't forgive her—Kathy had ruined her life, and she could never trust her again. So after mumbling on the phone, "I'm sorry, I really don't want to talk with you," she hung up.

70 x 7

Forgiveness is hard to give—especially when it's your neck in the noose. It's even harder when the person who fails you was someone you trusted.

When Peter asked Jesus, "Lord, how often shall my brother sin against me and I forgive him? Up to seven times?" (Matthew 18:21), Peter thought he was being saintly and generous.

He was shocked at Jesus' response, "Seventy times seven." It blew his thunder.

Scar Tissue

Ending a conflict is as hard as keeping New Year's resolutions. Old scars keep showing up red at the surface. But Scripture challenges us:

> *Let us therefore make every effort to do what leads to peace and to mutual edification.* Romans 14:19

And the writer of Hebrews encourages us with the way God forgives:

> *For I will forgive their wickedness*
> *and will remember their sins no more.* Hebrews 8:12

Our task is pretty clear . . . forgive and forget. Two very simple, but difficult words.

A Super-Human Dose

Who do you need to forgive? Why? Focus on the situation instead of the way you feel.

_____

_____

In your prayer time today, ask for God's forgiveness. Ask him to help you forgive yourself. Then contact the person you're having problems with. Be sincere and honest. Whether he or she accepts your efforts or not, you will know you have obeyed God. And you can commit the rest of the process to him.

Buddies No Matter What

☐ DAY ONE

Are Teachers (and Youth Leaders) Really Human?

Tia leaned back against the warm sofa and sniffed her steaming hot chocolate. *This is such a wonderful place*, she sighed, and snuggled into the creamy afghan. Coming here once a week was always worth the five-block walk—even in the middle of a winter like this one.

Mrs. Madge—no, Martha—she reminded herself (because that's what Mrs. Madge had asked Tia to call her) was a terrific lady. She seemed to care a lot about the high school kids she taught, more than just the average, everyday English teacher.

One day when Tia was feeling down in the dumps, Martha had noticed and had invited her over to her house after school. Martha thought of everything—even calling Tia's mom so she wouldn't be worried. During their talk, Tia discovered that Martha's husband had died a year ago and that she was pretty lonely.

At first Tia started visiting Martha once a week because— well—she felt rather sorry for her. But by December, things had changed drastically for Tia. She looked forward to their time together eagerly. Martha was the first older lady she really *wanted* to spend time with. Martha giggled over Tia's jokes, loved chocolate (especially gooey, half-baked brownies—Tia's favorite), and comforted her when she'd had a bad day.

For the first time in her life, Tia had a true friend she could share with—the good things as well as the bad. Martha understood. Tia only wished that they had found each other earlier.

Family Friends

Believe it or not, Tia and Martha aren't the only people in the history of the world to have an unusual relationship like that. Ruth and Naomi are another shining example. Naomi was Ruth's mother-in-law, but the old mother-in-law-not-getting-along-with-the-wife adage didn't come true here. Even as family members, they had an incredible friendship.

When Ruth's husband died, Ruth didn't leave Naomi to re-marry. Naomi was a widow, too, and Ruth stayed to be a loving support because Naomi was alone. This was unusual because outside of marriage, women had no place in that culture and they usually remarried. Because of her love for Naomi, Ruth endured being an outsider who had no protection from a husband.

God blessed Ruth for her friendship with the older woman. He gave her a wonderful home and husband, and blessed Naomi with grandchildren in her old age. Eventually, King David would be Ruth's great grandson!

Disciple-making

Paul the apostle had an unusual relationship with Timothy, whom he called "my beloved son." From reading Paul's letters in 1 and 2 Timothy, we can gather the following information about Timothy: he was a young man, a young Christian, timid and weak in his faith, and he wasn't physically well. Although they were miles away from each other, Paul wrote him two specific, lengthy letters encouraging him to stand strong in his faith and to rekindle his desire to serve God.

Bridging the Gap

Be friends with an older person? *You've got to be kidding*, you say. *I have nothing in common with them, and besides, they wouldn't understand me. Everybody knows that there is a generation gap between adults and teenagers.*

Perhaps there is a gap between *some* teens and *some* adults, but who says there has to be? There are a lot of things teens can learn from older people. Solomon, the world's wisest man, encourages teens to: "Listen to counsel and accept discipline, that you may be wise the rest of your days" (Proverbs 19:20).

And—surprise—there are many wonderful things that adults can learn from teens! Things like freshness, creativity, and a renewed zest for life, to mention a few. Just think what a terrific relationship you and an older person may be missing!

Write down the name of an older person with whom you'd like to pursue a friendship. (Or if you can't think of any, make a quick visit to a nursing home; you'd be surprised what spunky older people you'll find!)

———————————————————————

Now write down an activity that you could do for an hour with this older person. (It could be watching a video, cooking dinner together, looking over scrapbooks or photo albums, playing miniature golf, etc. The list is endless!) Give yourself one week to carry out your plan.

———————————————————————

If the idea of getting together with an older person scares you somewhat, here's some encouragement from Jeremiah:

> *"Do not say, 'I am only a child.'*
> *You must go to everyone I send you to*
> *And say whatever I command you.*
> *Do not be afraid of them,*
> *for I am with you and will rescue you,"* declares the LORD.
> Jeremiah 1:7-8

☐ **DAY TWO**

Hopscotch Is Kid Stuff

"**L**eah, I'm over here!" Jerry called and ducked behind the sofa. Leah chortled and scampered in his direction as quickly as her chubby five-year-old legs could carry her. The change in her was incredible. Two weeks ago, Leah had been abandoned on the steps of the Children's Care Center where Jerry worked after school. At first she just gently rocked on the floor with her fists clenched tight in her lap. She would sit head-down like that for hours. Then one day, Leah surprised Jerry by climbing into his lap. She looked at him, her blue eyes large with questions until he hugged her.

After that day, Jerry and Leah were buddies. Jerry spent even more time than usual at the center—as a volunteer. Somehow he surprised himself: *I can't believe it. I really care about these kids!*

His work was no longer just a job.

#1 in God's Eyes

It's easy to think that children are just kids—little rug rats, curtain climbers, things that get in our way and under our feet. But Jesus championed children.

When some children were brought to Jesus so that he could pray for them, the disciples rebuked them and were going to send them away. But Jesus said, "Let the little children come to me, and do not hinder them, for the kingdom of heaven belongs to such as these" (Matthew 19:14). Jesus didn't think that children were bothersome; he took time to love them and pray for them.

Who's the Greatest

When Jesus talked affectionately with his disciples, he called them "children." And he gave them a big lesson about faith. When the disciples rallied around Jesus, asking who the greatest one would be in the kingdom of heaven, Jesus brought a child and said:

> *"I tell you the truth, unless you change and become like little children, you will never enter the kingdom of heaven. Therefore, whoever humbles himself like this child is the greatest in the kingdom of heaven. And whoever welcomes a little child like this in my name welcomes me."* Matthew 18:3-5

By now, the disciples' mouths were hanging open in shock. *A kid—the greatest?* In those days, children were seen but not heard; they had no rights. So Jesus' teaching stunned the disciples.

But they were even more astonished when Jesus continued to say that children were so important that it would be better for someone to drown than hurt them!

Focus on Kids

How much time do you spend with children? In what situations?

_____

_____

Is the time you spend with children *voluntary* or something you feel that you *have* to do? (For instance, do you go to your five-year-old cousin's birthday party just because your Aunt Mabel is making you? Do you babysit just to get extra cash when underneath it all you *hate* kids?)

The next time you're with children, whether it's your choice or not, use your time to shine as a light for God. Remember—what you say and do is extremely important to a child because he will look up to you as a role model. Ask God to give you a loving heart for those kids around you.

☐ DAY THREE

You're Not Just My Brother

Four A.M. Nina paced back and forth in front of the bay window. Every two minutes, she parted the curtains and peered through into the rainy blackness.

Where is he? He should be here by now! she said out loud, but really more to herself.

It was Friday night—no, Saturday A.M. Nina was downright worried about her brother Joel. He was never late for anything, and he'd promised her a ride in the fiery red Camaro he'd just bought from another guy at college. Because it was Nina's sixteenth birthday tomorrow, he had promised to come from Rockville College just to celebrate.

Nina had tried to fall asleep on the couch, but she just couldn't—except for short snatches. Every time she heard voices, or a car door slam, she woke up with a start. But by 4:00, she was bolt awake. Visions of all the horrible things that might have happened to him flew through her mind—maybe he'd stopped to get gas, and someone stole his car, or—even more horrible—he'd fallen asleep at the wheel and *crashed*!

Nina thought back to all the times that they had fought as kids over toys and bicycles, and all the snotty comments that she had made when he started shaving and wearing cologne. And then, there was the time in fifth grade when she got really mad and bit him because he read her diary!

Still, in spite of their little fights, Joel was a great brother.

He really stuck up for her. *Kind of like a guardian angel,* Nina thought. Tears flooded her eyes.

Just then she heard a car door slam, and feet tripped up the stairs. *Joel!* Nina flung the door open and threw herself in her brother's arms.

For the first time in her life she realized that her brother was not just her brother—he was her friend.

Getting Along

Getting along together all the time isn't easy—especially when it's someone you *have* to be around all the time, like your family. Maybe it's that pesty younger brother who is always nagging you to fly kites with him (and you think that would be terribly un-cool). Or perhaps your younger sister gets into everything of yours—including your makeup, clothes, and personal journal! Or maybe your older brother is a real geek, and always does stupid things that really make you embarrassed.

Somehow, it's hard for that "brotherly love in Christ" kind of feeling to stretch to your own relatives. Maybe you even wish that you were born into a different family because your own is so weird!

Relative Power

The Bible gives us examples of people who were siblings and actually got along. Sure, it wasn't always easy, but they worked at their relationships.

Martha, Mary, and Lazarus are one such example. Martha and Mary were as different as you could be—Martha ran her legs off, trying to be the perfect hostess when Jesus came because she wanted to make sure things were just right; Mary, on the other hand, wanted to spend time with Jesus, so she hung around, right by his feet. And the result? Martha got mad at Mary, called her a lazy bum, and complained to Jesus about it. Undoubtedly, that wasn't the only sisterly incident like that. But even though Martha and Mary had lots of differences to work through, they shared two common loves—their brother Lazarus, and Jesus Christ. When Lazarus died, they both mourned his death and begged Jesus to heal him. What a family celebration there must have been when Lazarus walked out of his grave, with the graveclothes streaming from him!

Take Your Home's Temperature

1 John 3:10 warns, "This is how we know who the children of God are and who the children of the devil are: Anyone who does not do what is right is not a child of God; nor is anyone who does not love his brother." In short, God's saying that anyone who does not love his *brother*—and that includes siblings—is not his child. Christ calls us to treat our family members with love and respect, and wants us to keep harmony in our homes.

How do you treat your other family members? Make notes about your individual relationship with each one of them.

_____

_____

Is there a family member you are having problems with today? If so, jot down some ideas about how you can make peace with them.

_____

_____

During your prayer time today, read the following verses. Then ask God to help you live them out:

As a prisoner for the Lord, then, I urge you to live a life worthy of the calling you have received. Be completely humble and gentle; be patient, bearing with one another in love. Make every effort to keep the unity of the Spirit through the bond of peace. Ephesians 4:1-3

☐ DAY FOUR

People Who Grow on You—Like Fungus

F or weeks, Trent, the Geek of Scobey High, had been following Deanna around the school halls. No matter where
she was—class, her locker, right outside the girls' restroom—he showed up. With his wire glasses and pocket protector,
he was a real nerdy-looking character. So far Deanna had been
pretty good at avoiding him. But today her luck had run out.

I can't believe it! Deanna thought. *He's such a Geek! And why
does he have to sit at* my *lunch table?* Carefully she lowered her
orange tray with her milk and hamburger lunch special to the opposite end of the table. With a quick smile, she nodded to him
and eased into the attachable bench seat.

I'm so glad Mary and Susan are on their way. Phew! Deanna
sighed. But her relief was short-lived. In one clumsy act, Trent
scooped up himself and his tray and swooped down next to her.

Oh no! This is so-o-o embarrassing! Deanna screamed inside.
I'd rather kiss my brother than sit next to this guy! Her stomach flip-
flopped. This was the worst day of her life.

Unlovable People

If you were Deanna, what would you do? Loving or even *liking*
"unlovable" people is tough, especially when you feel like your
popularity is on the line. After all, why should you put yourself
out for a goof or a nerd, right? They can take care of themselves.

Jesus had to deal with unlovables. And even though he was perfect and sinless, he didn't always find it easy. He can really identify with you—whether it's the girl in your math class who never washes her greasy hair, or the smelly guy whose locker is next to yours (sometimes you feel like putting *Right Guard* in his locker when he's not looking).

Partial People

James 2:1-9 talks a lot about attitudes and playing favorites:

> *My brothers, as believers in our glorious Lord Jesus Christ, don't show favoritism. Suppose a man comes into your meeting wearing a gold ring and fine clothes, and a poor man in shabby clothes also comes in. If you show special attention to the man wearing fine clothes . . . have you not discriminated among yourselves, and become judges with evil thoughts? . . . "Love your neighbor as yourself" . . . But if you show favoritism, you sin and are convicted by the law as lawbreakers.*

The Recycler

When Jesus met an adulterous woman (see John 8), he didn't roll his eyes and dump her like some soggy, smelly piece of garbage. Boldly he took her aside and listened to her problems. And finally he comforted her and gave her a new chance at life. Jesus is a champion recycler. He takes "garbage" people and recycles them into something beautiful and useful.

Your Chance

Who are the "disposable" people in your school? Why do you see them that way? What specific thing can you do this week to help recycle one of them?

_____

_____

Make it simple and practical (it could be writing them a note, eating lunch with them, or even sharing a simple, friendly "hello"). Ask God to help you treat them as Jesus would.

☐ DAY FIVE

Sharks or Non-Christians?

Rhonda rounded the corner into her home room. Gratefully, she sank onto the cold wood chair and plopped her books on the floor. *Whew! I just got out of that one!* She sighed deeply. She was so glad that this was the end of the school year. And yet she was sad too—she really liked Dave. But lately things had been taking an unexpected turn.

Just then she heard a shuffling sound. There he was. Dave—Mr. Detective. "Hey, Rhonda. I'm really interested in this God stuff. Maybe I could go to your Bible study with you sometime?" Dave asked.

"Uh, yeah. That would be good," Rhonda blurted out. "But tonight's the last Bible study until fall."

"Great! I'll come tonight. I can even pick you up, O.K.?" Reluctantly, Rhonda agreed. After tonight, he'd think she was a religious freak, and he'd never want to talk with her again.

Which Do You Fear the Most?

Sharks or non-Christians? When a non-Christian approaches you, do you immediately scramble out of the water, or do you gulp and wait for the big bite? Sometimes you may feel like hanging a sign around yourself: DANGER—Beware of Non-Christians. But are they really as deadly as they appear? Will they warp you and make you forget your Christianity, or worse yet, laugh at you? Maybe you're afraid you would have to become their personal prayer warrior and pray them into getting saved. Or maybe you're worried you will accomplish nothing.

DANGER—Beware

Christ calls us to go into all the world and share the good news. That means sharing it through your life—your words and actions to your Biology lab partner. But God also warns us about the kinds of relationships we should *not* have with non-Christians.

Paul tells us that marrying non-Christians is out (2 Corinthians 6:14). But what about dating non-Christians? The Bible doesn't state in black and white that you should not date an unbeliever, but it does give directing principles. It talks about how the heart gets involved in relationships. And once you have that type of involvement, there is a lot of hurt in breaking it off—for both of you. Remember—the purpose of dating is not only to have fun and get to know more about others and yourself but to point you toward a possible marriage partner.

Us 1; Sharks 0

When Jesus died on the cross, he triumphed over Satan. He is only awaiting the final victory. And because we are his children, we can claim his power—even in relating to non-Christians:

> *No, in all these things we are more than conquerors through him who loved us.* Romans 8:37

> *Do not be afraid or discouraged because of this vast army. For the battle is not yours, but God's.* 2 Chronicles 20:15b

So, the battle is already won! All we have to do is show up every day for service, knowing that Christ has already triumphed. What could be better?

What kinds of relationships do you have with non-Christians? What could you do to draw a non-Christian friend closer to God?

_____

_____

In your prayer time, thank God that he has already won the battle. Rejoice that he already has the deathgrip on Satan's neck.

Jesus, the Ultimate Friend

☐ DAY ONE

Best-friend-of-the-year Award

*L*ori and Bridget did everything together—like band and drama club and going out on weekends. When Lori's boyfriend dumped her, Bridget was there. And Bridget and Lori cried together when Bridget's brother died in a car accident. They were two parts of the same heart; each could tell when the other one was hurting. And they could talk about anything, no matter how personal or embarrassing it was. They had perfect trust in each other.

Then Bridget's dad, who was an Army colonel, got transferred to Germany. Bridget and Lori cried together for a week. And then, suddenly, Bridget was gone. Lori clung to all the photos of the two of them together, and to the stuffed raccoon that Bridget had left her. But the empty feeling remained. How she wished Bridget were here! She was so lonely.

It's not fair, God! Lori cried out. *She was my best friend in the whole world. I'll never find someone like her!* Still, months later, Lori's heart ached for her best friend.

Friends with God?

All of us can really feel for Lori. We've all lost friends at one time or another. But there is one friend who will never leave us, who is continually there, who stands by our side no matter what. And just who is this Super-Friend? God.

Maybe you're saying to yourself, *You've got to be kidding! No one can be friends with God. God's the guy who grabs a big stick and whaps you if you're not good. And, besides, you can't touch someone who isn't there—who doesn't have a body.*

Let's take a look at God and see what kind of person he really is. The best way to take God's photograph and keep it continually with us is to read the Bible, God's camera. Then we will learn to see through the focused lens of his eyes.

Taking God's Photograph

What makes God a good friend? He has all the qualities (and many, many more) of great friends that we have studied in this book. Unlike human friends, God is always there:

> *Praise be to the . . . Father of compassion and the God of all comfort, who comforts us in all our troubles, so that we can comfort those in any trouble with the comfort we ourselves have received from God.* 2 Corinthians 1:3-4

Focus on You

Jesus is the best listening friend that anyone could ever have. And he can be yours. In fact, he's listening right now for you to tell him your needs and desires. And the best thing of all is that his telephone line is always open. You'll never get a busy signal. And there are no toll charges.

How do you picture God? Write down some of his qualities and what you think he looks like.

_____

_____

Do you see God as a friend? Why or why not?

_____

_____

In your prayer time today, ask God to show you what kind of a friend he is.

☐ DAY TWO

God Doesn't Keep His Fingers Crossed

Just when everything was starting to go great again, John felt like quitting. After two years, he had finally been interested in life again. A counselor had really helped him climb out of the depression that had seemed to bury him.

He knew that the peaceful, happy feeling was too good to last. Now it was happening all over again. He couldn't talk with his parents—they didn't pay much attention to him anymore. As far as they were concerned, John was "out of danger." He wouldn't embarrass them by trying to kill himself again.

John had met Steve at a volleyball game last summer. Steve was a cool guy, and he took a special interest in John. This year when John found out they'd be going to the same school, he was thrilled. He had finally found a friend.

Or at least he'd thought so. Last week he had shared his secret with Steve—what he had tried to do. Steve looked at him like he was some kind of weirdo. But that wasn't all. Steve had promised he wouldn't tell anyone, but he let it slip to a couple of the other guys. Now they were all being so nice that it was getting on John's nerves. He didn't want to feel like someone's ministry.

Not a Fair-Weather Friend

John found out the hard way that not all friends can be trusted. You never knew if they had their fingers crossed behind their backs or not. He was bummed; he figured there wasn't anyone in the world who wasn't a fair-weather friend.

All of us have felt like John did at some time in our lives. Maybe it was when your friend told a secret about you, or you found out the real reason why someone asked you out (it was on a dare called "Ask the Ugly Out Night"). You were humiliated.

God Is Upfront

There is a friend who knows all about us and still loves us anyway. He's never shocked. He knows about the lies we tell, or the key-chain we stole from the store, or the gossip we passed on about someone at school. He cares and understands when we've been wronged and we're hurting deep inside. Who is this friend? God.

> *Cast all your anxiety on him because he cares for you. And the God of all grace, who called you to his eternal glory in Christ, after you have suffered a little while, will himself restore you and make you strong, firm and steadfast.* 1 Peter 5:7, 10

As you open yourself up to God's love, you'll find new hope. Jesus accepts you just as you are. He understands your joys and hurts completely, even when others don't. When this understanding sinks in, you won't feel so lonely. It will give you courage and confidence to reach out to others.

Open Hands

How do you feel about the fact that God knows you intimately? (Nervous, happy, uh-oh, I'm in trouble . . .)

_____

_____

Try doing this exercise during your prayer time. Write down all the things that are bothering you today on a piece of paper. Crunch that paper into a ball in your fist. Then turn your palm up, still holding the wad of paper. Lift up your concerns to God in prayer; then turn your hand upside down and let the paper fall in the wastebasket.

That is how we should treat the things that are bothering us if we believe that God has control of everything.

☐ DAY THREE

A Loving Prize-Fighter

Tad swallowed hard. Sheila's words pounded over and over in his head: "Tad, I'm pregnant. What are we going to do?"

Sheila looked at him tearfully. Tad didn't know what to say. He never thought it would come to this—his parents would be shocked. After all, Tad was a P.K. (preacher's kid). Everyone thought he was raised in a perfect home. They couldn't figure out what had gotten into him the last two years.

Tad caused his parents nothing but embarrassment. On his sixteenth birthday, he'd gone out drinking with his buddies. When the cops pulled them over for speeding, they found an open beer in the car. Tad ended up in jail. His parents had picked him up, paid for his fines, and swallowed their pride.

But that wasn't the end. Tad was continually getting into a scrap of some sort. Last week in Shop class he'd punched a guy out, and his weepy-eyed mother had to come to the principal's office on her lunch break.

Then there was Sheila, who was really a good kid. Her parents didn't care much for Tad—they thought he was pond scum and forbade her to go out with him anymore.

How am I going to tell my parents? Tad agonized. He knew they were going to fly off the handle and sock him. *Well, I deserve it*, he thought.

But he was surprised at their reaction: "Son," his father said slowly, "What you have done is wrong, very wrong. We have given you many chances to straighten yourself out, but you haven't tried. This baby is yours, and you've got two choices: marry Sheila now, or help her out with expenses and then agree together to give up the baby for adoption. Those are your choices. Now, son, it's up to you." His parents turned and left the room. He heard his mother crying in the bedroom.

Round One

All of us know someone *somewhat* like Tad. Maybe it's the punk-rocker who goes to your Christian high school and ends up in the principal's office every day. Or perhaps it's Tom, the guy who smokes marijuana in the parking lot at lunchtime. Or maybe it's Marsha, who doesn't know where she belongs, so she ends up in every guy's backseat at some time or another.

Being a teen isn't easy, especially if your parents aren't supportive of you. Or maybe you think your mom has no brains at all, or your dad doesn't love you. And that leads you to rebel against them—in the way you talk, dress, and act. Sometimes you don't know *why* you rebel.

Birthright

Esau was somewhat like Tad. He treated his #1 son spot lightly. Genesis 25:34 tells the story of how Esau, home from a hunting trip, gave up his birthright (something permanent) for something temporary—stew for his hungry stomach.

In Bible times, the #1 son got special privileges, including the blessing of his father, for the rest of his life. He had his choice of everything. When Esau messed up, he could have gone to his father immediately and said, "Forgive me for picking something temporary over something eternal." But he didn't. Hebrews 12:15-17 tells us that Esau couldn't repent. He'd done it too many times.

Gung Ho for God

Sometimes we as Christians can be like Tad and Esau. We take our Christian commitment too lightly. When we do something wrong, we go to God flippantly and pray, "Father, forgive me for what I did," and then we go back and do it again. We abuse our knowledge that God is a forgiving God. We don't seem to think we will ever suffer the consequences of our sin.

Beware—there will come a time when, like Tad and Esau, it will be too late. There will be no chance to turn around. We may think we are getting away from our sin, but someday we will suffer its consequences, like Tad and Sheila.

But God wants us to be gung ho for him (see Psalm 51). What does this mean? That when we do something wrong, we not only *confess* our sin and tell God we're sorry but also *forsake* our sin—turn away from it and refuse to do it again. Because God loves us, he will confront us when we need to be confronted— even if our hearts are so hardened it takes a wallop instead of just a pin-prick.

Is there some area in your life where you have become hardened to doing wrong? A hidden place where you would be uncomfortable to bring Jesus with you?

_____

_____

A right relationship with God requires that you spend time with God in prayer and in reading his letter to you—the Bible:

> *All Scripture is God-breathed and is useful for teaching, rebuking, correcting and training in righteousness, so that the man of God may be thoroughly equipped for every good work.* 2 Timothy 3:16-17

Remember that you are God's prize. You belong to him.

NO ARTIFICIAL FLAVORS   100% Friendship ·

☐ DAY FOUR

A Down-to-Earth Friend

"Tony!" Tony turned just in time to see Doug dashing across his front lawn. "Bud, I'm glad I caught you. Do you want to go to a concert with me tomorrow? Dad's company got free tickets and he and Mom can't go," Doug wheezed, out of breath from his run.

"Sure, I'll go if you help me mow the lawn tomorrow. I promised I'd do it," Tony replied. Doug's fist tightened. He cared about Tony a lot, but sometimes Tony got to him. Tony always put conditions on everything so that other people would help him out with his work. Still, he really wanted to go to the concert with Tony, so he agreed.

The next night, Doug stopped over at Tony's house to pick him up for the concert. He was surprised to see Tony lounging around in his sweats.

"Oh!" Tony called. "I didn't know that the concert was to-night! Sorry! I can't go—I have to babysit for my little sister. Some other time."

Doug stormed out the door, furious. It was Tony's typical game. As soon as someone else helped him do his work, he can-celed out on doing what they wanted to do. Doug had had it up to his ears with him. That was Tony's last chance, and he'd blown it.

Condition Games

Has anyone ever played the game "Condition" with you? Things like—"I'll help you with your term paper if you'll come to my party tomorrow." "I'll like you if you get your hair cut the way I think you should." Or, "You really have to buy Levi's to be a member of our crowd." How does that make you feel? Usually downright mad. Maybe, like Doug, you feel used, or that people are just looking on your outside and not on your inside. They want you to conform to being who *they* want you to be—not who you really are.

God's Condition

Unlike humans, God only puts one condition on his friendship— that you accept him into your life unconditionally. He wants to come in and transform you into the best person you can be. He won't play popularity games with you. You're either totally his, or you belong to Satan. There's no living in between the two.

God loved us so much that he sent his son Jesus to take all our sins on his back. Jesus died in agony on the cross, nails threading through his hands and feet. But he did it out of love and compassion for each one of us. Jesus gave his life because he created us and loved us immensely:

> *Greater love has no one than this, that he lay down his life for his friends. You are My friends if you do what I command.*
> John 15:13-14

But the problem is, we've all sinned against God (Romans 3:23)—we want to go our own ways and do our own things. We deserve punishment, and yet Christ took it for us. What's our part? We need to make some choices: Believe that Christ died for us; tell him we're sorry for our sin, and that we want to be changed; and invite Jesus to be our Forever-Friend and Savior for the rest of our lives. And then we will have the best unconditional friend anyone could ever have!

True-Blue

Accepting Jesus as your guard and guide is the only condition to having him as the #1 True-Blue Friend who will never leave you.

Have you accepted Christ into your heart to be your guard and guide? If not, why not?

_____

_____

If you have accepted Christ previously, has he become your friend? Is your relationship with him exciting and constantly growing?

_____

_____

Christ longs for a close relationship with you. His one condition is that you accept him whole-heartedly as your #1 priority. Ask God to help make you willing to discover more about him. Make this your prayer:

> *I pray also that the eyes of your heart may be enlightened in order that you may know the hope to which he has called you, the riches of his glorious inheritance in the saints, and his incomparably great power for us who believe.* Ephesians 1:18-19a

☐ DAY FIVE

The Forever Friend

Brandon's heart ached. He couldn't believe it could hurt so much—even after five years.

Last weekend he had been invited to a barbecue with his friend Chaka's family. He had watched them all work together to get lunch ready—they were having so much fun. Brandon wished he had a dad. But his dad had left when Brandon was ten, and he could hardly even remember what his dad looked like. His mom had put away all the pictures in a locked drawer.

Just once, God! his soul cried. *Why can't I have a dad like that—just for one day!* Oddly enough, that Wednesday, his youth group leader talked about how God is not only our father—which Brandon had a hard time with because he thought all fathers were bogus—but our best friend. And even better, a forever friend who is always with us wherever we go.

Brandon hadn't prayed for a long time. Up till now, he really hadn't felt like God cared much about him, or he wouldn't have let his dad leave. But tonight, he prayed, "God, please be my dad. And, God, be my forever friend too. I really need one. Amen." He felt happy for the first time in months.

Best Friends

If you have accepted Christ into your heart and life, you are his child. It's pretty wonderful to have a best friend and daddy all wrapped up in one. God is proud to call us his own: "For not one of us lives for himself, and not one dies for himself; for if we live, we live for the Lord, or if we die, we die for the Lord; therefore whether we live or die, we are the Lord's" (Romans 14:7-8).

The Power in You

When Jesus left earth and ascended to heaven, he didn't leave us alone to fend for ourselves. He sent the Holy Spirit to help us every day (John 14:16-17). And he gives us a huge promise:

> "So do not fear, for I am with you;
> Do not be dismayed about you, for I am your God.
> I will strengthen you, surely I will help you,
> Surely, I will uphold you with My righteous right hand."
> Isaiah 41:10

The Best Is Yet to Come

God promised that the best is yet to come. Earth is like living in a garbage can compared to what's in heaven! And God is preparing a place for you. Just think—your very own room in the grandest mansion of all. But the best thing will be that you will be with your favorite friend in a place where no tears will fall. That's got to be a fairy-tale ending.

Jesus wants to be your forever friend. How can you draw closer to him?

_____

_____

Jesus is coming at a time no one expects. What do you need to do to get yourself ready to go with him?

_____

_____

Thank God today for the promises of his Word. Ask him to remind you constantly of his love and friendship for you.